RESTITUTION

An Important Message for the Overcomers

PRACTICAL HELPS FOR THE OVERCOMERS
BOOK 11

ZACHARIAS TANEE FOMUM

Unless otherwise stated, the Scripture quotations in this book are taken from the *New International Version* of the Holy Bible, the British Edition

Published by

A division of the Book Ministry of Christian Missionary Fellowship International

info@books4revival.com

I lovingly dedicate this book to

HENRY NING

The first fruit of our ministry in cameroon, in loving memory of that 29th day of September 1975, with great expectations for the future.

CONTENTS

INTRODUCTION

PREFACE

This book is the eleventh in a series titled "*Practical Helps For The Overcomers.*" The books in the series that have already been written are:

The thought of many is that when a person is saved, God forgives him and wipes away all the consequences of his past sins - that he is free. His freedom is so complete that he has no responsibility to rightly terminate with the past and to carry out restitution to those he wronged then. This book clearly examines that way of thinking in the light of the scriptures and sets out the Biblical message for those who have overcome and those who want to overcome.

If you do not want to reassess your life in the light of the Word of God, we recommend that you should forget this book completely and not bother to read it at all, for if you read it, you may find out that you have to carry out revolutionary restitution that will bring you to the crest of the wave of the Holy Spirit's move.

If you are an overcomer, or desire to become one, this is your book. May the Lord bless you as you read it.

We send this book out with prayer that the overcomers, in reading it, would become more conformed to their soon-coming Lord.

Yaounde, 21st December 1990.

Zacharias Tanee Fomum,
B.P. 6090 Yaounde,
Cameroon.

INTRODUCTION

It can be said that there are seven steps back to fellowship with God. They are:

1. A knowledge of sin
2. Sorrow for sin
3. Confession of sin
4. Separation from sin
5. **Restitution**
6. Forgiveness
7. Restoration

In our opinion, these seven steps are basic. The fact that many so-called believers and many believers today seem to live in an unending cycle of sin, confession of sin, some relationship with God and then confession of sin, some relationship with God and then back to sin, says that there is something fundamentally wrong somewhere. While we shall be treating this whole matter in another book, we feel compelled by the Holy Spirit within and the need of the saints around, to single out restitution and write urgently on it.

The reason for this is the fact that we have come to observe with increasing frequency, both in our lives and in the lives of multitudes, that where there was genuine, wholehearted and thorough restitution to God and to man for a sin committed, the person hardly went back to committing the same sin. In fact, it seemed easier to be delivered from other sins after restitution had been carried out for one sin. It would seem that the agony of restitution also leads to a new level of fellowship with God and a new hatred of sin, so much that the believer is more willing to co-operate with God and thereby work out that hatred of sin and departure from sin which the Holy Spirit has given him power for.

We are convinced that a return to Biblical restitution will bring a new day to the people of God. We have also read from the acts of God in the past that it was rare to see a genuine move of God that was deep and sustained, that was not accompanied by Biblical restitution.

We acknowledge that restitution is not all. Restitution must be preceded by a deep and thorough separation from sin, and then be followed by the seeking and receiving of forgiveness from the Lord, and finally, the seeking and receiving of restoration into the heart of God, for that is the God-ordained dwelling place for the believer.

We pray that the Holy Spirit will enable this message to be correctly understood and that He will soften the hearts of the saints to receive it with the fear of God in their hearts. We further pray that the Lord will not only lead multitudes of believers to carry out restitution for the past and to walk the way of restitution in the present, but that He will be glad to raise many who, having carried out restitution in their lives, will teach restitution and help others to carry it out.

It has been a privilege to include some testimonies by people who have obeyed the Lord and made progress in the life of restitution. We pray that such testimonies will make things clearer for you, and that they will encourage you to walk the way they walked and are walking. Glory be to the Lord. Amen.

SOME IMPORTANT ISSUES ON RESTITUTION

2

WHAT IS THE PURPOSE OF RESTITUTION?

There are a number of reasons that make restitution most desirable.

1. The first one is that it glorifies God by advancing His moral universe.
2. The second one is that it draws the person who restitutes nearer to the Lord.
3. The third one is that it ensures that people have what is theirs.
4. The fourth is that it lays the ground work for revival.
5. The fifth is that it provides fuel that causes revival flames to blaze.

Be a part of God's programme of restitution!

RESTITUTION: A CRISIS AND A PROCESS

Restitution is both a crisis and a process. The first time the person who has not been carrying out restitution is brought face to face with a major area of his life that needs restitution, he is face to face with a crisis. If he obeys the Lord and carries out restitution, then there is a breakthrough in his life. He has been through the crisis of restitution. From then on, he may now begin to walk the way of restitution; listening to the Holy Spirit ad obeying Him by carrying out any restitution that is shown to him, be it in a small or big matter. It would always be easier to obey in the future because the crisis obedience made it easier to obey in the future. As the person walks this way, he will be surprised by the many things and many attitudes about which he needs to carry out restitution and about which he was so blind in the past. As he walks this highway, his love for the Lord will deepen and his desire for Him will increase; his hatred for sin will increase and so will his love of righteousness.

That is the crisis and the process of restitution.

4

WHAT MAY NOT BE DONE IN THE NAME OF RESTITUTION

God has ordained that each person should be convicted by the Holy Spirit and should then carry out restitution. He has also ordained that He alone should be the Exposer of the sins of people. No one should expose the sins of another person while carrying out restitution for himself. He must in no way allude to the sins of others. No one should in the process of carrying out restitution confess to man things that should be confessed only to God. Sins in thought should be confessed only to God. What man knows about should be confessed to man and restitution carried out. The only way to carry out restitution for sins in thought is to put on the thoughts of the Lord. This should be done in the secrecy of the heart.

Restitution should not be used to ruin a life or lives. If a man committed adultery with another man's wife, he should not go and confess it to the person for he may ruin the marriage completely. Restitution should bless people and not destroy them. We repeat that God ordained restitution to bless the offended party and not to harm him. If the confessions that must accompany the restitution are likely to ruin those to whom a person wants to carry out restitution, then the process of restitution should be postponed and counsel sought. If you and some others committed a certain sin, you are to carry out restitution as if you sinned all alone. This is imperative.

It is relieving to confess one's sin to someone. We recommend this strongly. However, there are some sins that should be confessed to another person and not to the person who is directly affected by the sin. Again, we strongly recommend that spiritual counsel should be sought if the situation is delicate.

The flesh will stand in the way of restitution. No one should hold back from restitution because of his flesh. Let such a one go ahead and restitute and see the death, in experience, of the flesh.

Always ask, "*Who will be blessed by this restitution?*" If no one else will be blessed apart from you, then it is not restitution. Also ask, "*Who will be hurt by this restitution?*" If the party being restituted to would be hurt, then it is no restitution. God bless and lead you.

RESTITUTION IN THE OLD TESTAMENT

RESTITUTION IN THE OLD TESTAMENT—1

"If a man steals an ox or a sheep, and kills it or sells it, he shall pay five oxen for an ox, and four sheep for a sheep. He shall make restitution; if he has nothing, then he shall be sold for his theft. If the stolen beast is found alive in his possession, whether an ox or an ass or a sheep, he shall pay double."

"If a thief is found breaking in, and is struck so that he dies, there shall be no bloodguilt for him; but if the sun has risen upon him, there shall be bloodguilt for him."

"When a man causes a field or vineyard to be grazed over, or lets his beast loose and it feeds in another man's field, he shall make restitution from the best in his own field and in his own vineyard."

"When fire breaks out and catches in thorns so that the stacked grain or the standing grain or the field is consumed, he that kindled the fire shall make full restitution.

"If a man delivers to his neighbour money or goods to be kept, and it is stolen out of the man's house, then if the thief is found, he shall pay double. If the thief is not found, the owner of the house shall *come near to God, to show whether or not he has put his hand to his neighbour's goods.*

"For every breach of trust, whether it is for ox, for ass, for sheep, for clothing, or for any kind of lost thing, of which one says, "This is it", the case of both parties shall come before God; he whom God shall condemn shall pay double to his neighbour.

"If a man, delivers to his neighbour an ass or an ox or a sheep or any beast to keep, and it dies or is hurt or is driven away, without any one seeing it, an oath by the LORD shall be between them both to see whether he has put his hand to his neighbour's property, and the owner shall accept the oath and he shall not make restitution. But if it is stolen from him, he shall make restitution to its owner. If it is torn by beasts, let him bring it as evidence; he shall not make restitution for what has been torn.

"If a man borrows anything of his neighbour, and it is hurt or dies, the owner not being with it, he shall make full restitution. If the owner was with it, he shall not make restitution; if it was hired, it came for its hire.

"If a man seduces a virgin who is not betrothed, and lies with her, he shall give the marriage present for her, and make her his wife. If her father utterly refuses to give her to him, he shall pay money equivalent to the marriage present for virgins" (Exodus 22:1-17).

A MORAL UNIVERSE

God has created a physical universe. He has also created a moral universe. There are laws that govern the physical universe. One of these is the law of gravity. If a person decided not to believe in the law of gravity, the law is nevertheless existent and worse still the person will suffer the impact of the existence of the gravitational pull. There are also laws that govern the moral universe. The laws are altogether binding. A moral universe demands that there be consequences for the violation of moral laws. It is not enough for someone to say, "I have violated this law." He must suffer the penalty for that violation. He must do everything possible to bring things to the condition in which they were before he violated the law. He must do all that he can do to "unviolate" the moral law that he violated. No one can violate a moral law and just go away as if nothing has happened. The Lord demands that anyone who violates a moral law should do all that is possible to put things in order. It is not enough for a thief to acknowledge the fact that he has stolen. The thief has to do all that he can to ensure that the person from whom he stole is restored to the position in which he was before he was robbed.

THE RESTITUTION FOR THE THEFT OF AN OX OR SHEEP

The person who steals an ox or sheep and kills it shall pay five oxen for an ox and four sheep for a sheep. This is simple and clear. If you stole an ox or a sheep in the past, you should go and restitute it accordingly. The measure of restitution as given by the Lord is five oxen for one ox stolen, and four sheep for each sheep stolen.

The Lord also gave instruction that should someone steal an ox or a sheep, but has not yet killed or sold it, he shall pay double.

THE THIEF TO BE SOLD

The Lord saw that there would be thieves who would not be able to pay the fine for their theft. Are they to be allowed to go free because they were not able to pay back what they stole and the accompanying fine? No! The thief who could not carry out restitution, had to be sold! God has not permitted that thieves should be told, "You stole. You have repented but you are not able to pay. We forgive you. You are free. Pay nothing either now or in the future for your theft." Because God has not ordained that they be exempted from restitution, we refuse to exempt them from it. They must carry out restitution or be sold for their theft.

HARM DONE THROUGH CARELESSNESS TO BE RESTITUTED

The person who caused a field or vineyard to be grazed over or who let a beast loose so that it fed on another man's field, shall make restitution from the best from his own field and vineyard.

It is not permitted that through the carelessness of some, others suffer losses. Restitution must be carried out not only for evil or harm that was done intentionally but restitution has also to be carried out for harm that was caused as a result of carelessness or as a result of neglect! This applied to vine-yards if animals grazed them: animals that were not well taken care of, because if they had been taken proper care of, the harm would not have been done. The Lord was more or less warning against every form of carelessness. He was ensuring that the careful do not suffer in the hands of the careless!

RESTITUTION FOR IMMORALITY

A man who seduced a virgin who was not betrothed and lay with her was not allowed to say, "I am very sorry for the immorality which I have committed. Please forgive me." He was to do this and in addition, carry out restitution. He was to give the marriage present for her and make her his wife. He was not allowed to commit immorality and then give one reason or the other why he could not marry her. His act meant that he should be prepared to make her his wife. It meant that before a man committed such folly, he had to first ask himself, "Am I prepared to live with this girl as my wife?" If he answered "No" to that question, he was to put his immoral heart under control. If he did not put it under control and seduced her, then he had no choice, he had to marry her! When he married her, he was compelled never to divorce her (Deuteronomy 22:29).

If the father of the girl utterly refused to give her to him, he was to pay money that was equivalent to the marriage present for a virgin as punishment. He was thus to pay for his immorality! It was thus understood that the immoral were not allowed to merely confess their sin. There was a penalty to ensure that a person thought things over before he allowed himself to be carried away by folly.

RESTITUTION IN THE OLD TESTAMENT—2

"The LORD said to Moses: If any one sins and commits a breach of faith against the LORD by deceiving his neighbour in a matter of deposit or security, or through robbery, or if he has oppressed his neighbour or has found what was lost and lied about it, swearing falsely - in any of all the things which men do and sin therein, when one has sinned and become guilty, he shall restore what he took by robbery, or what he got by oppression or the deposit which was committed to him, or the lost things which he found, or anything about which he has sworn falsely; he shall restore it in full, and shall add a fifth to it, and give it to him to whom it belongs on the day of his guilt offering. And he shall bring to the priest his guilt offering to the LORD, a ram without blemish out of the flock, valued by you at the price for a guilt offering, and the priest shall make atonement for him before the LORD, and he shall be forgiven for any of the things which one may do and thereby become guilty" (Leviticus 6:1-7).

ALL SIN IS AGAINST THE LORD

We should always bear in mind that all sin is against the Lord! In the passage above it is said, "If any one sins and commits a breach of faith against the LORD by deceiving his neighbour." So he sins and he commits a breach of faith against the Lord when he deceives his neighbour. When we deal with man, we are dealing indirectly with God. When we are polite to man, we are being polite to God. When we are rude to man we are being rude to God. When we break our commitment to man, we are committing a breach of faith against the Lord. David said, "Against thee, thee only have I sinned; and done that which is evil in thy sight, so that thou art justified in thy sentence and blameless in thy judgment" (Psalm 51:4). The Lord Jesus said, "Truly, I say to you, as you did it to one of the least of these my brethren, you did it to me" (Matthew 25:40). Then He again said, "Truly, I say to you, as you did it not to one of the least of these, you did it not to me" (Matthew 25:45).

So a man could deceive his neighbour in a matter of any of the following:

1. Deceiving his neighbour in a matter of deposit
2. Deceiving his neighbour in a matter of security

He could also:

1. rob his neighbour
2. oppress his neighbour
3. have found what was lost and lied about it

In each of these things the Bible says, "He shall restore what he took by robbery, or what he got by oppression, or the deposit that was committed to him or the lost thing which he found, or anything about which he has sworn falsely, he shall restore it in full, and shall add a fifth to it, and give it to him to whom it belongs, on the day of the guilt offering."

When a man committed any of these sins he could do any of the following:

- Continue to lie that he had not sinned.
- Acknowledge that he had sinned and do nothing more about it.
- Acknowledge that he had sinned and confess his sin, and do nothing more about it.
- Acknowledge that he had sinned, confess his sin and beg the person against whom he had sinned to forgive him and do nothing more!
- Acknowledge that he had sinned, confess his sin and plead with the person against whom he had sinned to forgive him and in addition restore to the owner the full value of what he had stolen and end it there.
- Acknowledge that he had sinned, confess his sin and plead with the person against whom he had sinned to forgive him and in addition, restore to the owner, the full value of what he had stolen and add to it one-fifth of the value as a compensation for whatever hurts and inconveniences were caused him.
- Acknowledge that he had sinned, confess his sin and plead with the person against whom he had sinned to forgive him, and in addition, restore to the owner the full value of what he had stolen and add to it one-fifth of the value as a compensation for

whatever hurts and inconveniences were caused to him and in addition, bring to the priest his guilt offering to the Lord, a ram without blemish out of the flock valued at the price of a guilt offering and have the priest make atonement for him before the Lord and thus have forgiveness.

FULL FORGIVENESS

The Bible teaches that it is the seventh approach above that is the Lord's will. That approach causes a man to look at sin in the face and to confront the full measure of the harm done to man and to the Lord, and practical steps are taken to put things right with God and with man. The person who does this is at peace and is restored both to God and to man. This is only fair, since the sin committed hurt man and God, and it is therefore imperative that confession and restitution should involve the both parties that were hurt.

A SURPRISE!

Why is it that in our day most people stop their so-called repentance at the third approach? This must be the devil's lie, for the person goes away neither restored to God nor to man!

"Lord, grant us to face sin, and repentance from sin in the way that we should. This will satisfy your heart and help us to run away from sin!"

RESTITUTION IN THE OLD TESTAMENT—3

"And the LORD said to Moses, "Say to the people of Israel, when a man or woman commits any of the sins that men commit by breaking faith with the LORD, and that person is guilty, he shall confess his sin which he has committed, and he shall make full restitution for his wrong, adding a fifth to it, and giving it to him to whom he did the wrong. But if the man has no kinsman to whom restitution may be made for the wrong, the restitution for wrong shall go to the LORD for the priest, in addition to the ram of atonement with which atonement is made for him" (Numbers 5:5-8).

SIN IS BREAKING FAITH WITH GOD

In the passage above, we see clearly what sin is. It is breaking faith with God. The passage says, "When a man or woman commits any of the sins that men commit by breaking faith with the LORD." When a person is faithful, he holds the LORD in high esteem, holds God's law in high esteem and does not dishonour God by breaking His law. When he breaks the law of God, he has decided to break faith with God; he had decided to be unfaithful. He had given up faith in God. Sin, even in the smallest measure, is saying, "I do not believe that God is who the Bible says He is." Everyone who believes that God is who the Bible says that He is, cannot commit sins. When a person no longer believes that God is who the Bible says that He is, he can do anything and will do anything until he is restored into believing that the Lord is who the Bible proclaims Him to be.

Have you ever thought about the fact that:

1. any doubt,
2. murmur,
3. questioning,
4. impure thought,
5. impure touch,
6. impure word,
7. impure act,
8. disobedience,
9. and so on,

are acts that betray that faith with the Lord has been broken? Please think about it!

WHAT THE PERSON WHO BREAKS FAITH WITH GOD SHOULD DO.

The person who breaks faith with God should first of all be brought to the point where he sees himself as guilty. Unless he comes to terms with the fact that he has broken God's law and that this breaking of God's law is a serious matter, nothing much can happen to him. If he recognizes his sin and then confesses and forsakes it, he shall then confront the matter of restitution for the wrong he did.

In carrying out restitution as we saw before, there is restoration to man and there is restoration to God. In restoration to the man who has been wronged, there has to be full restitution of all that was damaged plus one-fifth. This had to be given to the person who was wronged. This meant that the person involved would know who he wronged and go to him and return 120% of what was taken or destroyed from him. This is binding.

NO ONE IS EXEMPTED FROM RESTITUTION

The Lord is most serious about restitution! It is rooted in the fact that He is a moral God, has created man as a moral being, and is in control of a moral universe. The moral God, the moral being of man and God's moral universe, demand that all moral issues be settled squarely. There can be no running away from them. If a man sins, he introduces a problem into God's moral universe. Moral issues have to be settled in the way He has ordained them to be settled. If man does what he chooses, in the way he chooses, at the time he chooses and decides to consider the issue settled, he deceives himself because nothing is settled until God accepts it as settled and He accepts as settled only what is settled according to His prescription!

Many people would say, "I need to carry out restitution but I can no longer trace the whereabouts of the person I defrauded." Others may say, "The firm I defrauded has already wound up its affairs. What do I do about restitution? Can I not just confess the sin to God and leave it there?" Another person may say, "The person I ought to restitute to is dead. Can I not forget the matter?"

Well, restitution is not something that one can forget. If there was no moral God who had created a moral man and a moral universe, it might be alright to think that way. Fortunately, there is a moral God, who has created both a moral man and a moral universe. He has prescribed how restitution should be carried out in the case where the right person to whom restitution should be carried out is not known and cannot be traced. His prescription is that, the person who has wronged another, "Shall make full restitution for his wrong, adding a fifth to it, and giving it to him to whom he did the wrong. But if the man has no kinsman to whom restitution may be made for the wrong, the restitution for wrong shall go to the LORD for the priest" (Numbers 5:7-8). So, if restitution cannot be made to the person who was wronged, it should be made to the kinsman of the person who was wronged, and if there is no kinsman, either because he is not known, or because he does not exist, the restitution for wrong shall go to the Lord!

This is the way to settle the matter God's way, as far as man is concerned.

SETTLEMENT WITH MAN IS ONLY A PART OF THE SETTLEMENT

It should be clearly understood that each time a man sins against another man, a two-fold sin has been committed. There is wrong against man and sin against God. There has to be confession of sin and restitution to man, and confession of sin and restitution to God.

So if a man steals, he should confess to the person from whom he stole and restore 120% of what was stolen to him. Then he should confess to God and offer the ram of atonement with which atonement will be made for him.

We know that we do not need to offer rams of atonement today since on the cross, the Lord Jesus offered atonement for all sin. However, each person who sins should bear in mind that he has sinned against God and man, and needs to restitute to God and to man. There can be no substitute for this!

RESTITUTION IN THE OLD TESTAMENT—4

"And the LORD sent Nathan to David. He came to him, and said to him, "There were two men in a city, the one rich and the other poor. The rich man had very many flocks and herds; but the poor man had nothing but one little ewe lamb, which he had bought. And he brought it up and it grew up with him and with his children; it used to eat of his morsel, and drink from his cup, and lie in his bosom, and it was like a daughter to him. Now there came a traveller to the rich man, and he was unwilling to take one of his own flock or herd to prepare for the wayfarer who had come to him, but he took the poor man's lamb, and prepared it for the man who had come to him." Then David's anger was greatly kindled against the man; and he said to Nathan, "As the LORD lives, the man who has done this deserves to die, and he shall restore the lamb fourfold, because he did this thing, and because he had no pity" (2 Samuel 12:1-6).

THE DOCTRINE OF RESTITUTION WAS WELL UNDERSTOOD

When the story of this unusual greed of the rich man who, while having very many flocks and herds nevertheless turned to the poor man and took his only lamb and prepared it for the visitor that he had, was told, David immediately saw the fact that the man had sinned terribly and deserved to die. In addition, he had to carry out restitution, which in his case would be a fourfold restoration of the lamb!

It is obvious then that the practice of restitution was common practice in Old Testament times. The people knew what the Word of God said. They took that Word seriously and they obeyed it with regards to restitution and with regards to the other aspects of the truth.

God expected that of them. They obeyed.

God's Word is available to us today.

Let us obey it!

Amen.

RESTITUTION IN THE NEW TESTAMENT

9

THE RESTITUTION OF ZACCHAEUS

"He entered Jericho and was passing through. And there was a man named Zacchaeus, he was a chief tax collector, and rich. And he sought to see who Jesus was, but could not, on account of the crowd, because he was small of stature. So he ran on ahead and climbed up into a sycamore tree to see him for he was to pass that way. And when Jesus came to the place, he looked up and said to him, "Zacchaeus, make haste and come down; for I must stay at your house today." So he made haste and came down, and received him joyfully. And when they saw it they all murmured, "He has gone in to be the guest of a man who is a sinner." And Zacchaeus stood and said to the Lord, "Behold, Lord, the half of my goods I give to the poor; and if I have defrauded anyone of anything, I restore it fourfold." And Jesus said to him, "Today salvation has come to this house since he also is a son of Abraham. For the Son of man came to seek and to save the lost" (Luke 19:1-10).

ZACCHAEUS' PAST LIFE

Zacchaeus was a chief tax collector. He was rich. The reputation that he established for himself as "a man who is a sinner" suggested that he used his office to make gains that were not legal. He himself confirmed that irregularity by his statement to the Lord. "If I have defrauded anyone of anything, I restore it fourfold." So we can deduce that part of Zacchaeus' problem was defrauding people.

The other part of Zacchaeus' problem was selfishness. He was blind to the needs of the poor.

ZACCHAEUS VIOLATED THE LAWS OF GOD

Zacchaeus violated the laws of God. He was not compassionate to the poor. He did not share what he had. He closed his eyes to the needy around him. He closed his ears to the cries of the poor. He knew that it was more blessed to give than to receive but he did not do a thing about it. He made wealth his god and consequently gave it the devotion of his heart. He did not bother as to how he was acquiring his wealth. When the poor came, he all the same defrauded them. His life was centred on himself and his goal was to make money.

ZACCHAEUS RECEIVED THE LORD AS HE WAS

Zacchaeus was still greedy, covetous and dishonest when he sought the Lord. He sought the Lord just as he was. Jesus decided to go to his house just as he was. Jesus actually went to his house just as he (Zacchaeus) was. Yes, Zacchaeus received the Lord joyfully without any change in his attitude to himself, to others and to money. The Lord did not demand that Zacchaeus should change until His light had penetrated him. Each one must come in contact with the Lord Jesus before he can decide whether or not he wants the salvation of God.

THE LIGHT OF JESUS SHONE IN ZACCHAEUS' HEART

All seemed to be going fine in Zacchaeus' life until the day that he met the Lord Jesus. Then all of a sudden, everything changed. He could no longer continue as he was. He was suddenly caught up with the burden, not only of enjoying the presence of the Lord Jesus, but also of getting right with God and man in everything possible, and as soon as possible!

He had received the Lord, and all of a sudden, money could no longer be his god. He had God and there was no place whatsoever for a god of any kind. He looked into the eyes of the Lord and that look made him see not only God but all the poor around to whom he owed a lot but was totally blind to before then. Yes, he saw the Lord and then he saw people as the Lord saw them. He saw the Lord and then he saw money as the Lord saw it. He then had the Lord's attitude towards people and toward money.

SEEING PEOPLE AS THE LORD SAW THEM

The question is, "How did the Lord Jesus see people?" The Lord saw the needs of people and had compassion on them. Let us look at a few incidents in the life of the Lord. In the gospel of Luke it is written that, "Soon afterwards he went to a city called Nain, and his disciples and a great crowd went with him. As he drew near to the gate of the city, behold a man who had died was being carried out, the only son of his mother, and she was a widow, and a large crowd from the city was with her. And when the Lord saw her, he had compassion on her and said to her, "Do not weep." And he came and touched the bier and the bearers stood still. And he said, "Young man, I say to you, arise!" And the dead man sat up and began to speak. And he gave him to his mother" (Luke 7:11-15).

He saw the widow, had compassion on her, raised her only son from the dead and gave him to her.

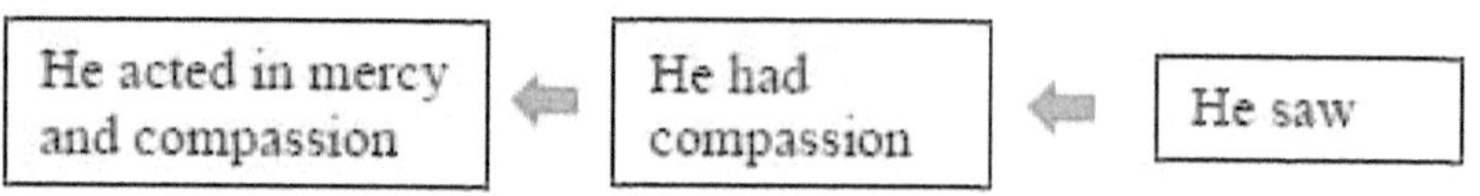

In another incident the Bible says, "The apostles returned to Jesus, and told him all that they had done and taught. And he said to them, "Come away by yourselves to a lonely place, and rest a while." For many were coming and going, and they had no leisure even to eat. And they went away in the boat to a lonely place by themselves. Now many saw them going, and knew them, and they ran there on foot from all the towns, and got there ahead of them. As he went ashore, he saw a great throng, and he had compassion on them, because they were like sheep without a shepherd, and he began to teach them many things. And when it grew late, his disciples came to him and said, "This is a lonely place, and the hour is now late; send them away, to go into the country and villages round about and buy themselves something to eat." But he answered them "You give them something to eat." And they said to him, "Shall we go and buy two hundred denarii worth of bread, and give them to eat?" And he said to them, "How many loaves have you? Go and see." And when they had found out, they said, "Five and two fish." Then he commanded them all to sit down by companies upon the green grass. So they sat down in groups, by hundreds and by fifties. And taking the five loaves and the two fish he looked up to heaven, and blessed, and broke the loaves and gave them to the disciples to set before the people and he divided the two fish among them all. And they all ate and were satisfied" (Mark 6:30-42).

First of all the Lord saw the apostles and had compassion on them because they were tired and there was so much pressure on them that they had no leisure even to eat. He acted in mercy and compassion by calling them apart to a lonely place to rest.

No sooner had He called them apart to rest than they were invaded by the multitude. He saw a great throng, and He had compassion on them, because they were like sheep without a shepherd; and He began to teach them many things. So, secondly, He saw the crowd in its hunger for the Word. He had compassion on the people because they were like sheep without a shepherd; and he began to teach them many things. Again, He saw, He had compassion and He acted.

As He was ministering to the crowd's need of spiritual food there arose a need of physical food. The disciples saw the crowd and decided that they did not want to become a part of the crowd's problem of the need of food. They recommended that they be sent away. They had no compassion on the crowd. The Lord Jesus saw the crowd, had compassion on them and decided to meet their material need and performed a miracle that met their need, "And they all ate and were satisfied!"

The Lord Jesus saw, had compassion, and acted to meet the need, whatever the need was!

ZACCHAEUS SAW PEOPLE AS JESUS SAW THEM - 1

When Zacchaeus received the Lord, and the light of the Lord shone through him, he too saw people as the Lord saw them. He first saw the poor. For the first time, he saw the poor! Of course, he had walked past many poor people, but he did not see them because his eyes were blinded by his greed. There is nothing as blinding as greed! Zacchaeus passed by the poor and looked at them but he did not "see" them. After he met the Lord, he saw! When he saw, he acted like the Lord Jesus! He had compassion on them and he acted in mercy and compassion to meet their need.

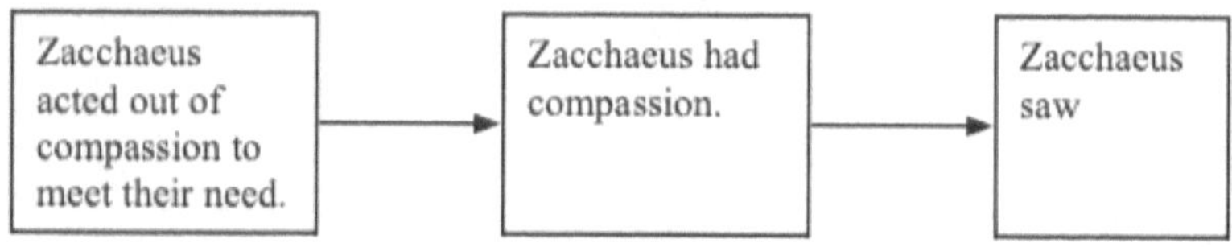

Zacchaeus realized then that all along, he ought to have shown compassion which he did not show. He decided at once that he had to do something about it. He decided to put 50% of all that he had gathered over the years into meeting the needs of the poor. He needed no one to tell him that. He had met the Lord Jesus and his eyes were open. His eyes were not only opened to the people and their needs. They were opened to what money was meant to be used for. Money was not meant to be kept - stored up. Money was meant to be given away so that it meets the needs of people. As he saw the needs of people and saw the real purpose for which the Lord allowed money to be used, he began to act as he ought to have acted.

It is a serious matter that Zacchaeus on his own decided to give away, not 10%; not 20%, not 30%; but 50% of his total wealth. He wanted to do the maximum that he could for the poor. He was restituting for his neglect of them for so many years in the past. If Zacchaeus had, say one billion francs, then in that one decision 500.000.000 francs, were given away and his wealth came down by that much!

When a person meets the Lord, he must face up to his thoughtlessness of the poor and do something big for them. When a person meets the Lord, he should face his responsibility to the poorest people on Planet Earth, those people who have not heard the gospel (for the lack of knowledge of God's way of salvation is the very fullness of poverty!) and act in a most compassionate way to meet their need. May I suggest that every rich person who meets the Lord should carry out restitution for having allowed so many people to perish while he accumulated money, by investing 50% of his total wealth into the work of the Gospel! This will manifest the fact that he has begun to see!

ZACCHAEUS SAW PEOPLE AS JESUS SAW THEM -2

Compassion is a must for those whose eyes are opened and therefore see as Jesus saw and as He sees. We have seen that Zacchaeus saw and did something about it.

There was another thing that Zacchaeus saw. He saw that people ought to have what is indeed their own. He knew that a part of his wealth was obtained fraudulently from people; that he had used his position to exploit them. He saw that he was in possession of money that God knew belonged to others. They might have been pressured into giving it to him, but he knew what God knew: that the wealth belonged to others! It was not his. He was not rich after all. He was illegally keeping what did not belong to him, while those to whom it belonged, were deprived of it. Knowing then that he was the false owner of their wealth, he decided to restitute by allowing them to have what was theirs. So the decision was taken: "Everyone that I have defrauded will have what is his returned to him!" The question then was, how much should be returned to each person? What guide was there? Did the Scripture provide guidance? Was God's written will about the matter known? He must have flipped through the whole Bible in his mind. Then his heart was arrested by the following verses, "If a man steals an ox or a sheep, and kills or sells it, he shall pay five oxen for an ox, and four sheep for a sheep" (Exodus 22:1).

Zacchaeus knew that he had used tact and guile to steal from people. He knew that he needed to restitute and that he should restitute five times or four times what he had stolen. He decided to restitute it fourfold. He knew what he ought to do and he decided to do it. He announced what he was going to do! He committed himself publicly to do it. Why did he do so? He committed himself publicly because he did not want to give the devil an opportunity to take him away from his decision. He knew that if he left the decision unannounced, the enemy might cause him to change his mind, but that if he announced it, it would not be possible to go back on the decision because there would be inward compulsion from the Holy Spirit and outward compulsion from those who heard him commit himself, to do what was right.

We had taken for granted that Zacchaeus' total wealth was 1.000.000.000 francs. Let us take for granted that 10% of his wealth was fraudulently earned, while 90% was honestly earned. Let us now see how much money Zacchaeus was left with after he carried out restitution to the poor and to those he had defrauded:

1. Total wealth = 100%
2. Percentage given to the poor = 50%
3. Percentage given to those he defrauded = 40%
4. Percentage of wealth left for him = 100 − (50 + 40) = 10%

This means that Zacchaeus' wealth now came down to 10% of what it was before he met the Lord Jesus. It means that, of the 1.000.000.000 francs that he owned, 900.000.000 francs had to be given away and 100.000.000 francs were left as his wealth. Meeting the Lord Jesus had cost him 900.000.000 francs in the first go, and more would be following!

Let us take for granted that Zacchaeus was a bit more corrupt and that 12.5% of his income was fraudulently earned, and only 87.5% was honestly earned. We know that he gave 50% to the poor and that he carried out a fourfold restitution. The situation then would look as follows:

1. Total wealth = 100%
2. Percentage given to the poor = 50%
3. Percentage given to those he defrauded = 12.5 x 4 = 50%
4. Percentage of wealth left for him after he had carried out full restitution was 100 - (50+50) = 0%

The reality is that, if Zacchaeus had defrauded people by twelve and a half percent of his total wealth, then meeting the Lord Jesus caused him total financial ruin. He became absolutely poor in material wealth!

There are people who say to others "Come to the Lord Jesus and all your problems will be solved." There is a sense in which this is true. For Zacchaeus, the problem of alienation from the Lord was solved; the problem of an eternity in the lake of fire was solved; the problem of an evil conscience because of the people defrauded was solved. However, a new problem was created. If he had defrauded people by one-eighth of his total wealth, then the problem of how to meet his daily needs was immediately created, and he had to confront a life of possibly living like one of the poor to whom he had closed his eyes in the past. He had to face the problem of possibly changing from a luxurious house to a poorer one; he had to face the problem of changing to a poor car or to no car at all; he had to face the issue of a new status in society!

Zacchaeus was not the same after he met the Lord Jesus! He was changed inwardly and he was changed outwardly. His wife felt the impact of the change. His children felt it and all who met him knew both from his outward appearance and inward outflow that something deep and far-reaching had happened to him!

THIS DAY SALVATION IS COME TO THIS HOUSE!

When Zacchaeus met the Lord, the Lord said to him, "Zacchaeus, make haste and come down, for I must stay at your house today." The Lord spoke and then the ball passed into Zacchaeus' court. Zacchaeus took the Lord to his house and the Lord waited for him to respond to Him. It is after Zacchaeus had announced his programme of restitution that the Lord Jesus spoke again, proclaiming the fact that salvation had come to Zacchaeus' house.

The restitution programme that Zacchaeus announced manifested the fact that his commitment to the Lord Jesus was deep and thorough. It manifested the fact that Zacchaeus was not in for half-measures. It manifested the fact that the idol that was on Zacchaeus' heart (money) had been overthrown and that Zacchaeus could now worship the Lord! Those who have the idol money on their hearts cannot worship the Lord in truth because their hearts are divided! The hymn writer understood the whole matter clearly and that is why he wrote:

> The dearest idol I have known,
> Whate'er that idol be
> Help me to tear it from Thy throne
> And worship only Thee.
> (SS and S N°583)

FULL SALVATION

The Lord Jesus said to Zacchaeus, "Today salvation has come to this house, since he also is a son of Abraham. For the Son of Man came to seek and save the lost" (Luke 19:10).

The question is, "What would have happened if Zacchaeus had come down from the tree, received the Lord Jesus, led him home but not announced his programme of putting things right and walking properly with God?" I think that the Lord would also not have proclaimed that salvation had come to his house. He would not have been saved. He would have been like some of those who began to follow Him, but fell away because of the full demands of discipleship. The Bible says, "So Jesus said to them, "Truly, truly, I say to you, unless you eat the flesh of the Son of Man and drink his blood, you have no life in you, he who eats my flesh and drinks my blood has eternal life, and I will raise him up at the last day. For my flesh is food indeed, and my blood is drink indeed. He who eats my flesh and drinks my blood abides in me and I in him. As the living Father sent me, and I live because of the Father, so he who eats me will live because of me. This is the bread which came down from heaven, not such as the fathers ate and died; he who eats this bread will live for ever." This he said in the synagogue as he taught at Capernaum. Many of his disciples when they heard it, said, "This is a hard saying; who can listen to it?" But Jesus, knowing in himself that his disciples murmured at it, said to them, "Do you take offence at this? Then what if you were to see the Son of Man ascending where he was before? It is the Spirit that gives life, the flesh is of no avail; the words that I have spoken to you are spirit and life. But there are some of you that do not believe. For Jesus knew from the first who those were that did not believe, and who it was that would betray him. And he said, "This is why I told you that no one can come to me unless it is granted him by the Father." After this, many of his disciples drew back and no longer went about with him. Jesus said to the Twelve, "Do you also wish to go way?" Simon Peter answered him, "Lord, to whom shall we go? You have the words of eternal life; and we have believed, and have come to know that you are the Holy One of God." Jesus answered them, "Did I not choose you, the Twelve, and one of you is a devil." He spoke of Judas the son of Simon Iscariot, for he, one of the twelve, was to betray him" (John 6:53-71).

Some of the disciples followed the Lord Jesus but at one point they found it too hard and so turned away and no longer followed Him! They gave Him up and gave up the salvation He had brought to them. Yes, they gave up the salvation He had brought to them for they went away from Him and no more walked with Him. Salvation is in Jesus! Away from Him is no salvation. Those who go away from Jesus have also gone away from the salvation of Jesus. Had Zacchaeus refused to carry out restitution, he would not have entered fully into the salvation of the Lord. He would not have been saved. The Lord Jesus carried out full salvation - salvation from sin in all its forms and from every manifestation and inclination of sin and to sin. Yes, Jesus saves to the uttermost those who turn to Him.

"SAVED, YET A THIEF?"

The Lord said, "Did I not choose you, the Twelve, and one of you is a devil?" He spoke of Judas the son of Simon Iscariot, for he, one of the Twelve, was to betray him" (John 6:70-71). Judas was called "a devil". Why? He was called a devil because he was a thief who did not repent and who betrayed Jesus in order to have money.

There is a sense in which every thief is a devil. How does this bear on the matter of restitution? The bearing is this: If a man defrauded anyone, he stole. He remains a thief until he has repented and restored what he stole. If such a person comes to the Lord and receives Him, he must go back and restore all that he stole. He might have stolen it by asking for a bribe, by asking for a favour that he should not have asked for and by using every means possible to acquire that which he should not have acquired. He has stolen and must restitute. If he does not restitute, he is a thief even if he claims to be saved. He is a devil, regardless of what he claims to be his experience in Christ. The law of God and the demands of God are immutable. The Bible demands that the thief who cannot restitute what he has stolen, should be sold for his theft. "If a man steals an ox or a sheep, and kills it or sells it, he shall pay five oxen for an ox, and four sheep for a sheep. He shall make restitution; if he has nothing then he shall be sold for his theft" (Exodus 22:1).

Are you a thief who claims to be saved? Go and carry out restitution! As long as you have not carried out restitution you are still in the old life, regardless of what you may claim.

Have you thought about the person you defrauded? Do you have compassion on him? If you do, go and carry out restitution. Remember also that what you have done to him has been done to God. You have stolen from God.

SPARING ZACCHAEUS?

The Lord Jesus stood by and watched while Zacchaeus carried out restitution that ruined his finances! Why did Jesus not spare Zacchaeus? Why did He not say, "Zacchaeus, I did not mean that you should go that far. I only wanted to test you. Give a tithe to the poor and do not bother about those you defrauded. It belongs to the old life and I have forgiven and cancelled that. Be at peace"?

If the Lord had done that, He would have been a proclaimer of false peace. He would have given someone aspirin when he needed surgery. He would have prepared him for spiritual death.

You have read the way that God wants restitution carried out. You have seen that the purpose for which God gives money to people is that it should be used to meet needs and not stored up. God evaluates riches in terms of what has passed through a man's hands, that is, the fruit of his labours that have been put into meeting the needs of those without the gospel and those with other needs. He considers that those who stock wealth for themselves are not only poor - they are wicked! We counsel you not to allow anyone to stand in the way of your carrying out restitution. He can deceive you now and help ease your conscience now but on that day you will stand alone to face your Judge. It is best for you to be reconciled to the Judge now by carrying out all the restitution that He demands so that on that day you shall be acquitted. Therefore, be wise. Act! Do not be disturbed by what it will cost you. What can you give in exchange for your soul? What can you give in exchange for a clear conscience? These are priceless - your soul and your conscience!

Be the lone man who dares to carry out full restitution. There are many who may claim to be walking with the Lord who have not bothered to carry out restitution! Do not imitate them. Do not be moved by what may appear to be their apparent spirituality or the apparent success of their ministries! God knows those who are His and He has counselled all who are His to depart from all iniquity. Be one such. Amen.

THE RESTITUTION OF THE RICH YOUNG RULER?

"And a ruler asked him, "Good Teacher, what shall I do to inherit eternal life?" And Jesus said to him, "Why do you call me good? No one is good but God alone. You know the commandments: 'Do not commit adultery, Do not kill, Do not steal, Do not bear false witness, Honour your father and mother," And he said, "All these I have observed from my youth." And when Jesus heard it, he said to him, "One thing you still lack, sell all that you have and distribute to the poor and you will have treasure in heaven, and come, follow me. But when he heard this, he became sad, for he was very rich. Jesus looking at him said, "How hard it is for those who have riches to enter the kingdom of God! For it is easier for a camel to go through the eye of a needle than for a rich man to enter the kingdom of God" (Luke 18:18-25).

MONEY IS DIRECTIONAL

Money is directional. The Lord Jesus said, "Do not lay up for yourselves treasures on earth, where moth and rust consume and where thieves break in and steal, but lay up for yourselves treasures in heaven, where neither moth nor rust consumes and where thieves do not break in and steal. For where your treasure is, there will your heart be also" (Matthew 6:19-21). He again said, "Fear not, little flock, for it is your Father's good pleasure to give you the kingdom. Sell your possessions, and give alms, provide yourselves with purses that do not grow old, with a treasure in the heavens that does not fail, where no thief approaches and no moth destroys. For where your treasure is, there will your heart be also" (Luke 12:32-34).

A man's treasure directs his heart. If he puts his treasure where the Lord wants it to be, his heart will go where the Lord wants it to be. If he obeys the Lord with regards to his treasure, he will also obey the Lord with regards to his heart and with regards to everything else in his life. If he disobeys the Lord about his treasure, he will also disobey the Lord about his heart and about every other thing.

A man should first of all obey the Lord about his wealth and then he will be able to obey the Lord about his

- sexual life,
- attitude to murder,
- attitude to theft,
- attitude to false witnessing,
- attitude to honouring his father and mother.

THE OBEDIENCE OF THE RICH YOUNG RULER

The rich young ruler obeyed the Lord's command about:

- adultery,

- killing,
- stealing,
- bearing false witness
- honouring father and mother.

It all looked so good! He sounded so promising. He looked so exemplary. The only problem is that adultery, killing and the rest are not directional. He obeyed in all these things but when that which is directional came along, he fumbled and was totally ruined. He passed all the tests except the test of freedom from the love of money and at that test, he gave up the Lord, gave up all that was deep and lasting and pursued the pathway of ruin.

If the man had obeyed the Lord about money first, money being directional, he would have been able to follow on and obey the Lord in all the other things that are not directional.

WHY DID JESUS WANT THE RICH YOUNG RULER TO SELL ALL AND GIVE ALL TO THE POOR?

Someone may ask, "Why did the Lord ask the rich young ruler to sell all and give to the poor before he could come and follow Him?" Jesus wanted him to transfer his wealth from earth to heaven. He wanted him to have treasure in heaven. Until that day, he had amassed all his treasure on earth and no treasure in heaven. The Lord wanted a transfer, not of a part but of all his treasure to heaven. The Bible says, "And Jesus looking upon him loved him and said to him, 'You lack one thing, go sell what you have, and give to the poor, and you will have treasure in heaven; and come follow me" (Mark 10: 20 - 21).

Jesus loved the young man and wanted the best for him. The best for the young man then and the best for every person then, and the best for every person now, is that the person should transfer all his wealth to heaven, for the only sure wealth is that which has been transferred. All the wealth that is already invested in the poor; all the wealth that is already invested in getting the gospel to the poor, is sure wealth. It is safe in the bank of heaven. All the wealth that has not been transferred, is really no man's wealth. There are a number of reasons for this:

1. Sudden death could bring a change in ownership. The new owner may waste it.
2. Thieves could soon become the possessors of this wealth.
3. Inflation could destroy it.
4. The sudden return of the Lord could render it totally useless.

So out of love, the Lord Jesus wanted all the young man's wealth to be transferred to the land of safety!

The other issue about it is the fact that this rich young man would not need the wealth. He was going to follow the Lord Jesus and the Lord would be responsible for all that he needed. Jesus was saying to him, "Transfer all your wealth to heaven now, and I will provide for all your needs for the rest of your life."

The Lord was not making a hard demand. He was making a loving demand. The young man stumbled on the Lord's love and went and perished!

There is another reason why the Lord wanted him to sell all that he had and give to the poor. The Lord Jesus wanted the rich young ruler to do in one go what he ought to have been doing all along. He had been blind all this while, all these years, to the needs of the poor and had his eyes open only to his own needs. That was wrong and the Lord wanted that corrected at once.

The Lord wanted him to carry out a form of restitution. The Lord had blessed all the poor around him by giving what He had for them to the young ruler. He was wealthy with what was meant for all who were around him. The Lord always blesses those around through the ones in whose hands He puts wealth. They are meant to hold it out for those in need. They are meant to tell the poor, "The Lord has made me your steward. He has given me this money to keep for you. Let me know what your needs are and I will use your money to meet them."

So, the rich young ruler had been an unfaithful steward. He had not served those he was meant to serve. He had kept as his own what he was given for others! He had hurt them by heaping up the money and things until he was very rich. He had great possessions but these possessions were actually not his. Initially, they were God's, for God owns everything. Then God allowed them to pass into his hands. God's possessions passed into the hands of the young man and became God's possessions in the hands of the young man. When they were in God's hands, they were to serve the purposes of God. When they passed into the hands of the rich young ruler, they remained God's possessions and their purpose remained to serve the purposes of God. God had now made the young man the custodian of His wealth and the servant of the poor around - the poor whom God wanted to have their needs met with His wealth.

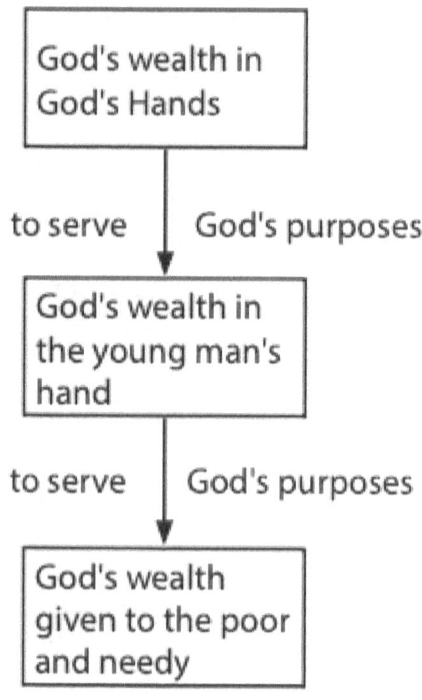

GOD'S FINANCIAL ORDER FOR THE RICH
YOUNG MAN

Unfortunately the young man made himself the end. That is why the undesirable adjective "rich" was added to his name.

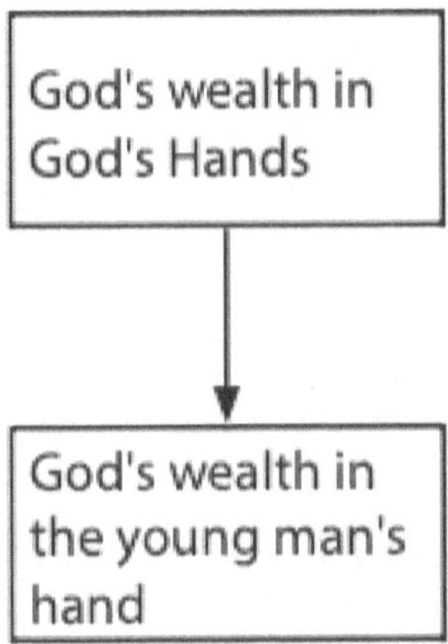

THE FINANCIAL ORDER THAT THE YOUNG
MAN ESTABLISHED FOR HIMSELF

This young man sinned grievously. He put aside God's financial order and replaced it with his own. God's financial order had the poor and needy as the terminal point of God's wealth. The young man overthrew this and established his own order that had himself as the end. He, therefore, cut supplies from where the Lord had meant them to reach and caused suffering that God never intended. He was an unfaithful steward and the Lord, in asking him to sell all that he had and give to the poor was just giving him a loving opportunity to be right again. No hardship was involved. The money never really belonged to the young man. It belonged to God and had to be used as the rightful Owner dictated.

If this young man were in his proper senses, he would have understood that the Lord was doing him a great favour. Unfortunately, he did not understand and did not want to.

He therefore, did not carry out the needed restitution. He jumped over the love of the Lord, jumped over the opportunity to carry out restitution, jumped over an opportunity to have treasures in heaven and jumped over an opportunity to follow the Lord Jesus and fell into the permanent grip of Satan and thus prepared himself for eternity away from the Lord, in hell! I do hope you will not be as foolish as he was!

OWNED BY GOD, GIVEN BY GOD, TO BE USED FOR GOD

All possessions belong to God

The Lord said,

> *"The silver is mine, and the gold is mine, says the LORD of hosts"* *(Haggai 2:8).*

> *"The earth is the LORD's and the fulness thereof, the world and those who dwell therein" (Psalm 24:1).*

> *"For every beast of the forest is mine, the cattle on a thousand hills" (Psalm 50:10).*

All possessions that man has have been given to him by the Lord so that he may be a steward of these

The Bible says,

> *"You shall remember the LORD your God, for it is he who gives you power to get wealth" (Deuteronomy 8:18).*

And if you have not been faithful in that which is another's, who will give you that which is your own?" (Luke 16:12).

All possessions are to be used as the Owner (God) wants them used. They are to be used for Him

The Bible says,

"This is how one should regard us, as servants of Christ and stewards of the mysteries of God. Moreover it is required of stewards that they be found trustworthy" (1 Corinthians 4:1-2);

"Calling ten of his servants, he gave them ten pounds, and said to them 'Trade with these till I come" (Luke 19:13)

"Sell your possessions and give alms" (Luke 12:33).

The Lord owns all that you have. All that you have has been given to you by the Lord and you are to use it for Him and at His command. This being so, those who:

- hoard,
- accumulate,
- store up for many years,
- close their eyes to the needy around,
- are living in luxury while others are dying in dire need,
- are "rich" which means those who are keeping what they

should have given away, are true enemies of God.

ALL THAT YOU OWN IS GOD'S AND SHOULD BE USED FOR HIM.

If you look around you will notice from continent to continent, nation to nation, city to city, family to family and from person to person, that the gifts of God are not evenly distributed.

Whether it is:

- money,
- food,
- beauty,
- talents,
- spiritual gifts,
- mental abilities,
- and so on,

God has varied His distribution of them. His aim in so doing is to cause the one who has one thing to share what he has, and the one who is in need of one thing to receive it from the one who has it. This is to be carried out at family level; then at city, national and finally, continental levels. If man understood this and practised it, the suffering in the world now should end.

At the spiritual level, the one who has received a revelation of some aspect of the truth is not to consider himself special. He is to consider himself as a servant of those who have not yet received that aspect of the truth. He is to bear with them, teach them patiently with much prayer and fasting until all of them come to a knowledge and an experience of that truth. He is not to withdraw from the rest and start something of his own so as to have freedom to practise that truth. He is to fast and pray and labour with much patience until there is a breakthrough! It is only in this way that the purpose of God for giving him that aspect of the truth can be fulfilled. Any aspect of the truth that leads to division of those who belong to the Lord betrays the fact that an aspect of the truth has been wrongly understood or wrongly applied. The same applies to all

1. gifts,
2. successes,
3. promotions,
4. and so on.

All are the Lord's, all are given by the Lord and all are to be used to serve the Lord's interest, that is, for the common good. Each one should understand that what the Lord has given him is for the blessing of others. The apostle Paul wrote, "To each is given the manifestation of the Spirit for the common good" (1 Corinthians 12:7).

THE NEED FOR RESTITUTION

If you have not been using your talents, gifts, opportunities, blessings, successes, and so on, for the good of all; if you have been using them to create a gap between you and the others; if you have been using them without reference to the will of the One who gave them to you, then you erred. You should repent and you should carry out restitution. You should confess your sins to God, and if need be, to man and then you should go back, and with more zeal than you have ever manifested in your life, carry out restitution by working doubly hard at putting what you have received at the disposal of all. This is restitution and it is a must for all who will go all the way with the Lord.

The rich young ruler went away and perished. May God grant you the grace to do what he failed to do and thereby lay up treasures for yourself in heaven.

Glory be to the Lord! Amen.

RESTITUTION TODAY

11

GOD HAS NOT CHANGED!

We have said that God is a moral God, and that He has created a moral man and a moral universe. Part of the implication of this is the fact that He could not demand honesty in the Old Testament and not demand it in the New Testament. He could not demand honesty during New Testament times and be unconcerned about it in the twentieth century! He could not demand truth then and demand falsehood today. He could not insist then that people should carry out restitution so that the rightful owners may have what is theirs, and today permit that people should not carry out restitution and consequently reap where they did not sow!

Restitution is for today! This message concerns you! You will confront the repercussions of this message today and you will confront them again at the Judgment Seat of Christ. You should do something about them. You should do all that you must do about them.

Although there are many situations in which full restitution cannot be carried out, because the moral damage caused by sin cannot be fully and completely restituted, each person must be able to say to God, "My Lord, I have done all that I think I could do to carry out restitution in this matter. I am willing to do any additional thing that you show me. My Lord, please speak to me. My Lord, I am your servant; speak to me. I will obey." The Lord will surely speak to such a person!

12

A FALSE APPLICATION OF THE CROSS

There is a false application of the cross today. That application says or implies that because the Lord Jesus has died on the cross, everything that a person did before he believed has been cancelled by the cross and consequently he is free to enjoy the new life in Christ without bothering to put right, heal or straighten out all the disaster that he had caused by his former way of life. Of course, this is a false doctrine, for it contravenes God's government in a moral universe. Such a doctrine leaves a thief to live in the luxury of the things that he stole while "praising God and walking happily with Him", while the person from whom he stole, is living in abject poverty, being deprived of what he rightly laboured for!

The cross does what man cannot do to re-establish his relationship with God and man, and in no way absolves a man from what he can and must do to re-establish his relationship with God. At the cross God did what only He could do.

Man must now do what he can do and must do, to put things right with God and man.

The easy believism, so characteristic of our day, that offers cheap solutions for deep moral issues, and takes no regard for God's moral nature and the moral nature of God's man and God's world, is not to be accepted by all who have truly encountered the King of the cross.

GOD CANNOT PRACTISE FALSEHOOD

When man sinned, God did not say, "Although man has sinned and though My laws demand that the Saviour should go into the world and die on a cross in order to buy man back to Myself, that pathway is too costly. First of all, it would mean that I shall be separated from My beloved Son for thirty-three years. That will be painful - very painful. Secondly, it will mean that My Son would have to put aside divinity and take on Himself human form, become a man, learn obedience and become obedient even unto death on the cross. Now, that would be too costly and too degrading. I will forget about the reality of the cross. I will just decree that man has been forgiven. In that way I would spare Myself and My Son, and nevertheless, have man brought back to fellowship with Me."

If God had done that, He would have deceived Himself and man would not be reconciled to Him. Man would have remained lost! Because God did not practise falsehood, He paid the full price of man's reconciliation to Him by the actual death of His Son on the cross. Man is consequently reconciled to Him. It was costly, but it was effective. The result is that God has man back in fellowship with Him, the Son can and does see the fruit of the travail of His soul and is satisfied and will be satisfied; and man has been delivered and is being delivered from the kingdom of darkness and being restored to the Lord.

GOD CANNOT ACCEPT FALSEHOOD!

The God who cannot practise falsehood cannot accept it. He cannot fellowship with anyone who, while violating the moral principles of restitution, continues to pretend to be His. Let me be honest with you: Unless you carry out all the restitution that the Holy Spirit shall open and has opened your eyes to as you read this book, your fellowship with God will be broken! You can deceive yourself but God will not become a part of your deception. This is not a light matter, for the Bible says, "But as for the cowardly, the faithless, the polluted, as for murderers, fornicators, sorcerers, idolaters, and all liars, their lot shall be in the lake that burns with fire and sulphur, which is the second death" (Revelation 21:8). "But nothing unclean shall enter it, nor any one who practises abomination or falsehood, but only those who are written in the Lamb's book of life" (Revelation 21:27).

THE POWER OF SMALL THINGS

A woman gave two small coins into the treasury of the Lord and earned the honour of having given more than all those who put in money - even large sums of money.

The need to take God seriously is of paramount importance and is illustrated by the following story: "And behold, a man of God came out of Judah by the word of the LORD to Bethel. Jeroboam was standing by the altar to burn incense. And the man cried against the altar by the word of the

LORD, and said, "O altar, altar, thus says the LORD, "Behold, a son shall be born to the house of David, Josiah by name; and he shall sacrifice upon you the priests of the high places who burn incense upon you, and men's bones shall be burned upon you.' And he gave a sign that same day, saying, "This is the sign that the LORD has spoken: 'Behold, the altar shall be torn down, and the ashes that are upon it shall be poured out.'" And when the king heard the saying of the man of God, which he cried against the altar at Bethel, Jeroboam stretched out his hand from the altar, saying, "Lay hold of him," and his hand which he stretched out against him, dried up, so that he could not draw it back to himself. The altar also was torn down, and the ashes poured out from the altar, according to the sign which the man of God had given by the word of the LORD. And the king said to the man of God, "Entreat now the favour of the LORD your God, and pray for me that my hand be restored to me." And the man of God entreated the LORD; and the king's hand was restored to him, and became as it was before. And the king said to the man of God, "Come home with me, and refresh yourself, and I will give you a reward." And the man of God said to the king, "If you give me half of your house, I will not go in with you. And I will not eat bread or drink water in this place, for so was it commanded me by the word of the LORD, saying, "You shall neither eat bread, nor drink water, nor return by the way you came.'" So he went another way, and did not return by the way that he came to Bethel.

Now there dwelt an old prophet in Bethel. And his sons came and told him all that the man of God had done that day in Bethel; the words also which he had spoken to the king, they told their father. And their father said to them, "Which way did he go?" And his sons showed him the way which the man of God who came from Judah had gone. And he said to his sons, "Saddle the ass for me." So they saddled the ass for him and he mounted it. And he went after the man of God, and found him sitting under an oak; and he said to him, "Are you the man of God who came from Judah?" And he said, "I am," Then he said to him, "Come home with me and eat bread." And he said, "I may not return with you or go in with you, neither will I eat bread nor drink water with you in this place; for it was said to me by the word of the LORD, "You shall neither eat bread nor drink water there, nor return by the way that you came.'" And he said to him, "I also am a prophet as you are, and an angel spoke to me by the word of the LORD, saying, "Bring him back with you into your house that he may eat bread and drink water." But he lied to him. So he went back with him, and ate bread in his house, and drank water.

And as they sat at the table, the word of the LORD came to the prophet who had brought him back; and he cried to the man of God who came from Judah, "Thus says the LORD, "Because you have disobeyed the word of the LORD, and have not kept the commandment which the LORD your God commanded you, but have come back, and have eaten bread and drunk water in the place of which he said to you, 'Eat no bread and drink no water;' your body shall not come to the tomb of your fathers'" And after he had eaten bread and drunk, he saddled the ass for the prophet who he had brought back. And as he went away a lion met him on the road and killed him" (1 Kings 13:1-24).

God had spoken to him clearly. He put aside the word of God and obeyed the lies of man, and that was the end for him! You have been warned. It was a small matter of eating food and having a drink once. He disobeyed and lost everything, including his life!

There may be small restitutions to make. If that is the case, you only carry them out for your own good, or disobey to your own undoing!

13

RESTITUTION OF THINGS TO GOD

There are the property laws of God in the Bible. One of those laws says, "All the tithe of the land, whether of the seed of the land or of the fruit of the trees, is the LORD's; it is holy to the LORD. If a man wishes to redeem any of his tithe, he may add a fifth to it. And all the tithe of herds and flocks, every tenth animal of all that pass under the herdsman's staff, shall be holy to the LORD" (Leviticus 27:30). "And the LORD said to Moses, "Moreover you shall say to the Levites, 'When you take from the people of Israel the tithe which I have given you from them for your inheritance, then you shall present an offering from it to the LORD, a tithe of the tithe'" (Numbers 18:25-26). "For I the LORD do not change, therefore you, O sons of Jacob are not consumed. From the days of your fathers you have turned aside from my statutes and have not kept them. Return to me, and I will return to you, says the LORD of hosts. But you say, 'How shall we return?' Will man rob God? Yet you are robbing me. But you say, 'How are we robbing thee?' In your tithes and offerings. You are cursed with a curse, for you are robbing me, the whole nation of you. Bring the full tithes into the storehouse, that there may be food in my house; and thereby put me to the test, says the LORD of hosts, if I will not open the windows of heaven for you and pour down for you an overflowing blessing. I will rebuke the devourer for you so that it will not destroy the fruit of your soil, and your vine in the field shall not fail to bear, says the LORD of hosts. Then all nations will call you blessed, for you will be a land of delight, says the LORD of hosts" (Malachi 3:6-12).

It is clear then from the Bible that ten percent of a man's income belongs to the Lord. If a person should defraud the Lord by not giving Him the required tithe, he has to carry out restitution. He should calculate what he owes the Lord, add to it one fifth and then give it to the Lord. This is basic[1].

The person cannot say, "I have stolen from the Lord for the last three months. I repent. I will steal no more. From this month I will begin to give a tithe to the Lord." If he does that he will be saying that a thief can say, "Forgive me for I have stolen. Forget the things I stole. From now on, I will steal no more. Congratulate me on my decision." Such a thief should be sent to prison!

Are you owing God a tithe or some money or property that is legitimately His? Go and pay your debt to God. Go and carry out restitution to Him. You have no choice in the matter if you want to walk in truth and honesty before Him and with Him.

---

[1] It is understood that new believers will be taught to give to the Lord as soon as they believe. If they do not know God's

mind about giving to Him, they cannot be held responsible. However they are held responsible from the day they know that they should give to the Lord. If they have to restitute, they shall restitute what they have not given to the Lord from the time they first knew they should.

14

RESTITUTION OF PROMISES MADE TO GOD

In the New Covenant, a man's promise to the Lord or to anyone, has the same power and the same standing as an Old Testament vow. The words of a believer are final and they are binding. What comes out of a believer's mouth and enters the moral universe of God, is most serious. It has the full strength of a deep commitment. The warning of Scripture is,

> *"Guard your steps when you go to the house of God; to draw near to listen is better than to offer the sacrifice of fools; for they do not know that they are doing evil. Be not rash with your mouth, nor let your heart be hasty to utter a word before God, for God is in heaven and you upon earth, therefore let your words be few. For a dream comes with much business, and a fool's voice with many words. When you vow a vow to God, do not delay paying it; for he has no pleasure in fools. Pay what you vow. It is better that you should not vow than that you should vow and not pay"* (Ecclesiastes 5:1-5).

If you made a promise to the Lord to:

1. Fast,
2. Pray
3. Give a certain amount,
4. Witness,
5. Forgive someone
6. Sacrifice something for the gospel,
7. Not marry in order to serve Him,
8. Leave your job and serve Him,
9. Break a certain relationship,
10. Build a certain relationship,
11. Not go to a certain place,
12. Go to a certain place,
13. Go to someone,
14. Not go to someone
15. Eat something
16. Not eat something
17. Dress in a certain way
18. Not dress in a certain way
19. And so on.

You should keep your promise. If you made the promise and forgot it you should carry out restitution. You should ask for forgiveness and go back to doing what you promised you would do. If you promised the Lord that you would fast five days each month last year and you failed to do so, you should repent and carry out restitution. You should fast for six days every month from now until you have fasted for twelve months. If you promised that you would give 20% of your income unto world evangelism but never translated your words into action, then you should repent and carry out restitution. You should calculate how much you owe Him, add 20% to it and pay it to Him. If you promised to pray for the unsaved for one hour each day, and you have not done so for the last two years, you owe the Lord 2 x 365 prayer hours plus one fifth of that number which is a total of 876 hours. You should plan how you are going to pay this debt. It may mean that you begin to pray for three hours every day to catch up. It may mean converting your nights into prayer times. Your week-ends may have to be invested in prayer. Your holidays may have to be invested in prayer. It will be costly but there is no way out. You made a promise to the Lord of heaven. He heard it. The angels in heaven heard it. The wicked one also heard it. You do not want to give the Enemy the opportunity to say that God's children treat Him lightly.

An aspect of the fear of the Lord implies that a person does all that he promised the Lord that he would do. Failure to do so, is mocking God.

THE BIBLE COMMANDS THAT VOWS BE PAID

The Bible insists that vows made to the Lord be paid. "When a man vows a vow to the Lord, or swears an oath to bind himself by a pledge, he shall not break his word, he shall do according to all that proceeds out of his mouth" (Numbers 30:2). "Offer to God a sacrifice of thanksgiving and pay your vows to the Most High" (Psalm 50:14). "Make your vows to the LORD your God, and perform them" (Psalm 76:11). "I will come into thy house with burnt offerings; I will pay thee my vows, that which my lips uttered and my mouth promised when I was in trouble" (Psalm 66:13-14).

The men of the Bible paid their vows at great price to themselves. They determined that whatever their lips had uttered before the Lord should be fulfilled and they kept their word. One example that is striking is that of Jephthah. The Bible says, "Then the Spirit of the LORD came upon Jephthah, and he passed through Gilead and Manasseh, and passed on to Mizpah of Gilead, and from Mizpah of Gilead he passed on to the Ammonites. And Jephthah made a vow to the LORD, and said, "If thou will give the Ammonites into my hand, then whoever comes forth from the doors of my house to meet me, when I return victorious from the Ammonites, shall be the LORD's and I will offer him up for a burnt offering." So Jephthah crossed over to the Ammonites to fight against them, and the LORD gave them into his hand. And he smote them from Aroer to the neigbourhood of Minnith, twenty cities and as far as Abel Keramim, with a very great slaughter. So the Ammonites were subdued before the people of Israel. Then Jephthah came to his home at Mizpah and behold his daughter came out to meet him with timbrels and with dance; she was his only child, besides her he had neither son nor daughter. And when he saw her, he rent his clothes and said, "Alas, my daughter you have brought me very low, and you have become the cause of great trouble for me, for I have opened my mouth to the LORD and I cannot take back my vow." And she said to him, "My Father, if you have opened your mouth to the LORD, do to me according to what has gone forth from your mouth, now that the LORD has revenged you on your enemies, on the Ammonites." And she said to her father, "Let this thing be done for me; let me alone two months, that I may go and wander on the mountains, and bewail my virginity, I and my companions." And he said, "Go" And he sent her away for two months; and she departed, she and her companions, and bewailed her virginity upon the mountains. And at the end of two months, she returned to her father, who did with her according to his vow which he had made. She had never known a man. And it became a custom in Israel that the daughters of Israel went year by year to lament the daughter of Jephthah the Gileadite four days in the year" (Judges 11:29-40).

INTEGRITY

Jephthah was a man of integrity before God. People of integrity say with him, "I have opened my mouth to the LORD, and I cannot take back my vow." O that such men would rise up in the church of the First Born! Jephthah's daughter knew the Lord, feared Him and loved her father. Those words, "My father, if you have opened your mouth to the LORD, do to me according to what has gone forth from your mouth", show the depth of her consecration to the Lord.

Do you know that what you have opened your mouth to the Lord about cannot be taken back? That is integrity. Are you one who would insist, and always insist regardless of what it may cost you, "If you have opened your mouth to the LORD, do to me according to what has gone forth from your mouth?"

Jephthah kept the word that had gone out of his mouth to the Lord, at great cost. You go and do likewise. Amen.

15

RESTITUTION OF THINGS TO MAN

The domain is very wide but we shall mention only a few areas. We commend you to the Holy Spirit who will lead you the whole way, for He knows all that you need to restitute. We want to say that restitution is an on-going thing. There are things that the Lord will show you today as areas needing restitution. If you faithfully carry out restitution in that area, He will show you the next thing and if you obey, He will show you the next. It will go on that way until He has done a deep and lasting work in you. Even after that deep and lasting work has been carried out in you, you will realize that the Holy Spirit will continue to work in you to bring you to repentance and restitution. As long as you live and as long as you are prone to sin, knowingly and unknowingly, you will continue to be led in the way of restitution.

MONEY

1. Do you owe anyone money and even though you can pay him, you have not paid him? You are banking your own money while preventing him from having his own. You are in the grip of greed. Repent and carry out restitution.

2. Are you a rich person? Do you have much money stored up for many years while people around you are dying of starvation, poor health, no educational facilities and above all, when there are people on Planet Earth who have not yet been reached with the gospel and who would be reached if you gave away some of your money? If that is the case, you should repent and carry out restitution.

3. Did you find money dropped somewhere and you picked it and used it for yourself? You are a thief! You should carry out restitution. If you can no longer find out who the owner of the money was, you should add 20% to it and give it to the Lord.

4. Have you ever received a bribe? If you have, you are a thief. Go and carry out restitution.

5. Did you abuse the office that was entrusted to you? You went out on missions that were not absolutely necessary, just because you wanted to use the opportunity to make additional income. You sinned. You should carry out restitution. Or you went on mission and even though you were housed and, or fed, you still claimed the total mission allowance as someone who was neither lodged nor fed. You are a thief. You should carry out restitution. Perhaps you used the cars, the telephone, the personnel, the

paper, the pens, the envelopes, the time; of your employer, to carry out your private affairs. You are a thief. You must carry out restitution.

6. Could it be that you filled in false information as you were declaring your taxes and thereby paid lower taxes than you should have paid? You are a thief, repent and carry out restitution.

7. Did someone give you some money to keep and then he forgot about it and you too decided to forget? You are a thief. Repent and carry out restitution.

8. Did you borrow money from someone and because the person forgot or would not ask you, you too decided to forget? You are a thief. Repent and carry out restitution.

9. Could it be that someone intended to give you say, ten thousand francs, but mistakenly gave you twelve thousand francs and you just kept quiet about it? Well, you are a thief. Repent and carry out restitution.

10. Do you, while selling things, expose the best ones on top and hide the worst ones below and consequently have someone pay for them with the understanding that all are as the ones exposed? You are a cheat. You should repent and carry out restitution.

11. Do you give the impression that you have no money (whereas you have) and thereby obtain undue sympathy from the people around? If that is the case, you are dishonest. Repent and carry out restitution.

12. Do you confess that you have no money, whereas you have, for fear that you may be asked to help someone who is in need? You are dishonest. Repent and carry out restitution.

13. Do you use your employer's time to carry out a second job and thereby earning a second salary? If that is the case, you should repent and carry out restitution.

14. Do you use the things that belong to your boss to make gifts, causing him to think that you are carrying out publicity while causing the person to whom the gift is given to understand it to be the fruit of your labours? You are dishonest. You should repent and carry out restitution.

15. Did you live with someone while you were not being paid and had him pay for all your expenses, but when you began to earn your salary, you did not think it fit to recompense him? Rather, you made arrangements to move away as soon as possible? If that is the case, please repent, and carry out restitution.

16. Did you receive money from someone or from some people to put into a particular project but did not put it in that for which it was designated and rather used it for yourself? You are dishonest. Repent and carry out restitution.

17. Did you use the advantage of your relationship to someone in a high position to obtain a job for which you are not the best candidate, and in that way caused the one who was best qualified to be disappointed? You should repent and carry out restitution.

18. Is your employment based on a false diploma? You should repent and carry out restitution.

19. Did you change your age in order to be qualified to obtain your current job? You should repent and carry out restitution.

20. What areas of financial dishonesty are there in your life? Could it be that you were given the money of the Lord to keep, and through carelessness it was stolen, and you did nothing about it? You should repent and carry out restitution. Did you cause two different sources to pay for the same bill and in that way made money by corrupt practice? If that is the case, you should repent and carry out restitution.

21. Have you withheld the money that you should give to your relatives who are in need? You should repent and restitute if that is the case.

22. Have you withheld the money that you should give to the poor, the widows, and the fatherless? If that is the case, you should repent and carry out restitution.

16

RESTITUTION IN THE REALM OF LOVE TO MAN

1. Have you deprived your wife or husband of love? You should repent and carry out restitution.

2. Have you caused the wife or husband of someone to be deprived of love by unlawfully absorbing her or him in yourself? If that is so, you should repent and carry out restitution.

3. Have you starved your children or parents of love? You should repent and carry out restitution.

4. Did you promise some girl that you would marry her and after some time you changed your mind, found someone else and married her while the first one remained stranded? Do you realize that you are the one responsible for the fact that she later on, out of frustration did any of the following:

- Got married to someone she did not love, out of frustration? That marriage is not working and you are the one responsible for its failure.

- Became a prostitute? You are the one responsible for her sin.
- Became the mother of illegitimate children? You are responsible for her fate and that of those children.
- Committed suicide? You are responsible for her death.
- Taught women to treat men wickedly? You are responsible for all the evil that such women cause and responsible for all the pain that the men have had to suffer.
- Decided that God does not love her and turned her back completely to God? You are responsible for her perdition.

You will have to carry out restitution that depends on what the situation has become. The first thing is that you will have to look out for her and repent to her with abundant tears, pleading with her to forgive you for the evil you caused her. You will have to do everything to help mend her broken heart and broken life. You will need to invest time and money into it while ensuring that you are not trapped into further sin. Yes, you will have to carry out restitution. If she is jobless you might have to help her financially. If she has a bastard, you may have to help with the material and perhaps emotional needs of the child. There is much that you will have to do and perhaps keep doing until you have reduced, to a minimum, the wounds caused by your sin.

5. Did you divorce your wife or husband? If you did, then you will have to carry out restitution. Ask God and He will show you what you must do.

6. Did you put on character traits that have made you undesirable to your partner? Perhaps you have become

- dirty,
- fat,
- aggressive,
- untidy,
- purposeless,
- unspiritual,
- lazy, and so on.

It does not matter which. You have sinned. You have to repent for causing him to have to live with such a dirty, fat, aggressive, untidy, purposeless or unspiritual person. You will have to repent and carry out restitution. You will have to beg him to forgive you for the inconvenience or problem that you are to him and decide that you will do everything that can be done so that by a certain date these undesirable traits have all been removed from your person and personality. You should ensure that you do not only remove the negative traits but that you adorn yourself with the positive traits that your partner wants. This is restitution.

7. Have you treated your wife as a thing? You have not bothered about her:-

a) material needs:

- good housing,
- good clothing,
- good kitchen utensils
- good furniture,
- pocket money, and all else that she may need that can be provided for from your income.

b) emotional needs:

- remaining slim so that she can appreciate your looks,
- being always clean so as to please her,
- being tender,
- never using hard or harsh words,
- appreciating her efforts to please you,
- paying attention to improvements in her looks,
- giving her occasional gifts,
- remembering her birthday and buying her a gift,
- remembering your wedding anniversary and making it a day apart,
- helping her to come out of spiritual poverty,
- and so on.

In any area where you have failed, you should repent and carry out restitution. The same should apply in any area in which you have backslidden and in any area where your present level of performance is still where it was last year or five years ago.

8. Have you treated your children as things? Have you been hard and wicked? Have you wounded them by treating your wife (their mother) harshly and shamefully? Have you failed to supply their material needs - clothing, food, fees, books, transport, and so on? Have you failed to love them - give time to each one: to understand him, sympathize with him and encourage him? These and all other areas of care are your debt to your children. If that debt has not been paid then you should repent to them and carry out restitution. In addition, you should repent to the Lord for treating His precious gifts to you with such contempt, and in addition, offer to the Lord a thank offering because, in His love, He has not taken the children away from you by calling them

home to Himself because of your poor performance as a father. Such restitution is necessary. It is basic. It is a must.

9. Have you lied about someone? You have thereby destroyed his reputation before man. You should repent and go and confess to him that you lied about him. You should ask him to forgive you and you should go to the people you lied to and confess to them that you lied. Then you should go about telling all the positive truth that you can about the person. This is costly but you have no choice. You can obey the Lord and continue with Him or refuse to restitute and part with Him.

10. Have you exposed someone's weakness to others in order to belittle him? You should go and repent to him if you did. You should ask him to forgive you. Then you should go exposing the virtues of the person to as many people as you can. That is restitution. Do not say that you cannot find any virtue in him. If you say that, you are indirectly criticising his Master. Can you afford that? In addition, to say that you cannot find any virtue in him, is saying that you have lost your power to see. Cry out to God for sight. Meanwhile, repent and carry out restitution.

11. Have you harboured resentment against a member of:

- your family,
- another family,
- your quarter,

Have you harboured resentment against someone in your:

- town,
- city,

- nation,
- continent or planet?

If that is so, you must repent and carry out restitution.

12. Do you hate people of a certain

- colour,
- size
- shape,
- tribe,
- city
- nation or
- continent?

If that is the case you should repent and carry out restitution. Do not say that you do not understand because the hatred is natural. It is not natural. It is supernatural. It is from Satan. The Son of God overcame him on the cross. Use the name of Jesus to overcome him and overcome his work of producing hatred, dislike or indifference in you against those people. Repent and carry out restitution.

13. Do you hate, dislike, or avoid people of a certain,

- religion,
- denomination,
- sect,
- and so on?

You should repent. If they are in error, you are to love them to the truth. If they are in darkness, you are God's light for their darkness. How can you take the light away from them? How does your attitude manifest conquering love? How does your attitude testify to the triumph of the Crucified? Did He not come out of heaven to seek those of another religion? Has He not committed to us the ministry of reconciliation? How can you ever reconcile them to God if you would not love them and go to them? If they are to meet the Lord at the cross, does it not demand that you and they be found together at the cross? You should repent. Yes, you should repent. The death of Christ on the cross tore down barriers. Carry out restitution. Tear the barrier of pride, reserve, self, and so on and press your way to them and by the grace of God, you will all soon be children of the Lord and the existence of another religion, denomination and that sect will soon be no more. This is a must, for to fail to carry out this type of restitution will be to stand in the way of the cross.

14. And more as the Holy Spirit will lead. Amen.

AT CROSSROADS?

17

IS IT TOO COSTLY?

You might have followed the message in this book and understood what God would have you do, but the question may linger in your mind as to whether it is not too costly. Well, I do not know. We have not been called to discuss whether it is too costly or not. We have been called to obey. If the Lord has spoken to you then you should stop discussing the cost and begin to obey.

You might be asking if you cannot forget about the need to restitute and continue your walk and your work with God. The truth is that having read this message, you will never be able to be the same. You are now at crossroads. You can obey the Lord and move into a higher dimension of fellowship with God or you can disobey Him and begin the descent. We can illustrate it as follows:

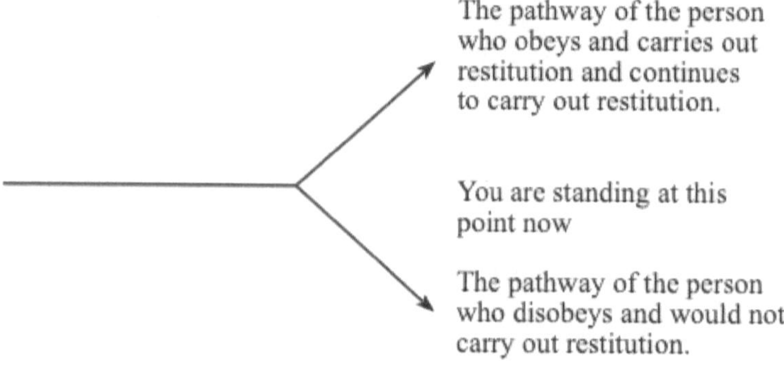

AT CROSSROADS

The Lord Jesus taught saying,

"Enter by the narrow gate; for the gate is wide and the way is easy, that leads to destruction and those who enter by it are many. For the gate is narrow and the way is hard, that leads to life and those who find it are few" (Matthew 7:13-14).

We do not promise you that the way of restitution will be easy. If we made such a promise we would be making a false promise for the Lord Jesus said that the way will be hard. He certainly knew what He was talking about. We agree with Him that the way of restitution is hard. We however, say that the Lord Jesus will come along with the one who is carrying out restitution and help him along the hard way and that the companionship of Jesus will see him through, first in the first crisis of restitution and then in the issuing life of restitution. So, do not be discouraged. You will not be alone. You will be in the company of the Lord Jesus and He knows that way. When it becomes too hard for you, He will not only hold you by the hand but He will lift you and bear you on his shoulders, and thereby guarantee your success. In Him, success is guaranteed! Hallelujah!

18

THE OVERCOMERS !

The Lord intended that the whole Church should be made of overcomers. Unfortunately, many believers have settled for God's second best. They have settled on the wrong side of the Jordan because they are afraid of the risk of stepping into the Jordan, and the further dangers of forcing out the Canaanites from the land. Only a few are prepared for the overcoming life. Only a few are prepared to become overcomers. The Lord says to those ones,

1. "To him who conquers I will grant to eat of the tree of life, which is in the paradise of God" (Revelation 2:7)
2. "He who conquers shall not be hurt by the second death" (Revelation 2:11).
3. "To him who conquers, I will give some of the hidden manna, and I will give him a white stone, with a new name written on the stone which no one knows except him who receives it" (Revelation 2:17).

4. "He who conquers and who keeps my words until the end, I will give him power over the nations, and he shall rule them with a rod of iron, as when earthen pots are broken in pieces, even as I myself have received power from my Father; and I will give him the morning star" (Revelation 2:26-28).

5. "He who conquers shall be clad thus in white garments, and I will not blot his name out of the book of life, I will confess his name before my Father and before his angels" (Revelation 3:5)

6. "He who conquers, I will make a pillar in the temple of my God, never shall he go out of it, and I will write on him the name of my God, and the name of the city of my God; the new Jerusalem which comes down from my God out of heaven, and my own new name!" (Revelation 3:12).

7. "He who conquers, I will grant him to sit with me on my throne, as I myself conquered and sat down with my Father on his throne" (Revelation 3:12).

The Lord has so much in store for the overcomers. Do you see why you should overcome at any cost to yourself? Listen, the Lord Jesus paid the whole price in everything and overcame. You, too, should pay the whole price in everything, including restitution and overcome.

Glory be to the Lord. Amen.

19

HELPING SOMEONE TO CARRY OUT RESTITUTION

One thing that a careful study of restitution would show is that the Holy Spirit is the best person to lead a person into repentance. No one should be forced to carry out restitution because no one can really force another to restitute. By forcing someone, the outward motions may be carried out while the heart remains unmoved. The teaching of the Bible on restitution should be taught. The teaching should be preceded by deep praying that the Lord would move. During the teaching, earnest prayers should be made to God that He would cause the Holy Spirit to move hearts to obedience. After the teaching, there should be even greater labours and greater wrestles with the Holy Spirit, pleading that He will move men and women to carry out restitution. This is because no one can carry out restitution unless the Holy Spirit opens his eyes to see.

If the Holy Spirit moves a person to enter the crisis of restitution, he may need help. This help may make him carry out a more complete restitution. It will be necessary for a mature believer who has carried out restitution to stand with him in prayer and in sorting out what needs to be confessed to whom, what needs to be restored to whom and what new attitudes need to be developed to replace those that have been abandoned.

If monies are to be paid back that are not available, the mature believer will counsel on how this one can be "sold for his theft" and yet be free to earn money and redeem himself.

My prayer to the Lord is that, since a mighty revival will soon be upon us, it is important that there be raised in the Churches, an increased number of saints who have been through a deep and thorough crisis of restitution and are walking the way of restitution, so that when the Spirit shall be poured out in a mighty way, the many new believers who will be added to the Body of Christ will have many competent spiritual guides so that the revival will accomplish all of God's ends for it.

Please pray with me that God should answer the above prayer. Please prepare to be one such guide by rendering total and radical obedience to the Holy Spirit in any area in which He may be demanding restitution from you today. God bless you exceedingly. Amen.

20

IN CONCLUSION

We accept the crisis of restitution and enter into it today, by carrying out the most outstanding restitution that the Holy Spirit is placing His finger on today. He is placing His finger on a serious matter and the consequences will be far-reaching. We say "Yes" to Him and we declare with Zacchaeus that we are going to do the things we must do, today. If we cannot do them today, we confess aloud to people and tell them what we are going to do and then seek the earliest opportunity to do it.

We accept the process of restitution, committing ourselves to carry out restitution at once in any area of our lives in which the Holy Spirit will cause His light to shine.

By walking in both the crisis and the process (or the way) of restitution, we satisfy God's heart. Amen.

TESTIMONIES

21

RESTITUTION-1

It was time to prepare for the next academic year. Among the things I needed, was drawing equipment. One of the items in the drawing equipment was a compass set. I went to the bookshop to buy one, but the seller, instead of selling it to me, told me to come back in the afternoon. This disturbed me because I could not understand this reluctance to sell an article that was available and for which I had ready cash to pay. However I did not argue. On returning in the afternoon, he took me outside and gave me the compass; but the sum I gave him was inferior to the normal price. Though I was not happy with what I was doing, I was afraid to refuse. I knew that this money was not going into the cash desk of the bookshop.

About two years later, I accepted Jesus Christ as my Lord and Saviour. Shortly afterwards, I completed my studies and picked up a job. When one day my eyes fell on the compass set, it recalled memories of how I obtained it and my conscience knew no rest from that moment. However, I had nobody to counsel me on this matter because as a believer at the time, I was isolated and not sharing the fellowship we enjoy today as an assembly.

I felt that I had to do something about it, but I did not know exactly how to go about it. I finally thought of going to reveal what I had done to the bookshop owner. I was afraid because I thought of being thrown in prison. As I realized that there was no other alternative, I thought it wise to wait for my first salary so that if need be I could pay a good amount of money so as to free myself from an eventual difficulty. But I was working in the Public Service and the first salary could delay for months before coming. One afternoon, full of fear, I took the compass set and went to the bookshop. I asked to see the owner of the bookshop and he was there. At first he was discourteous, but he granted me audience all the same.

I explained everything to him, telling him the circumstances through which I acquired the compass set that I held before him. I could not even recognize the person who sold it to me as he wanted to know the person. I could sense that he was disappointed, maybe, due to the realization that he had been deceived by one of his employees. He came back to himself a few minutes later and said to me, "You came to reveal this matter to me so that your work may go on smoothly..." He encouraged me to feel free and told me to go away.

My fear left and I was happy; happy for having been forgiven before God and before man. I realized that before God lays a burden on any heart, He first of all ensures that all will go well. He wanted me to walk on a pathway that is straight! That brought me even closer to Him. I came to know Him as being strict and just but also as being very good.

RESTITUTION–2

I was a regional manager in a town of our nation called Garoua. In this capacity I was in charge of the funds in our service. I was a child of God and the Lord had sustained me all along, such that I had a good testimony among my neighbours.

However, situations arose whereby my covetousness became manifest in all its forms such that I no longer bothered about using office equipment for personal ends.

One day I was transferred after being promoted. One of the workers in charge of financial matters came and drew my attention to a certain problem. One of the articles we had ordered some months earlier had not been delivered, and a similar amount of money was available for us to order something equivalent. That is when my heart could not resist temptation. Instead of placing an order for service equipment, I made one for my personal use. My conscience reacted instantly against it, but I hardened my heart. After I took my new duties, what I had done kept troubling me. As the word of God was preached very powerfully at a meeting, I was convicted of sin. Not knowing what to do, I spoke to a brother who gave me a piece of advice. I collected the money corresponding to the price of the articles I had taken and went to the financial service department to expose what I had done. There, the reimbursement I wanted to make was accepted. It was then that my heart was liberated.

But I also had to confess this sin to my boss. I made him know that despite the high opinion he had of me, I could also be involved in a case of fraud as the one I was confessing to him. He listened attentively and told me that everything was settled, but that in future, I should not take such a big risk for such small sum of money. However, he did not reject me.

When I left his office, I could once more look up to the sky and at the horizon. I could not understand how far my heart could have strayed away from the Lord. I humbly came back to God, regretting with all my heart and feeling miserable because of what I had done, thus breaking His heart and frustrating the Holy Spirit.

Following what I experienced, something of the fear of God has been created in my heart. I stagger most often and even stumble, but by His grace He keeps me to Himself. I should also point out the fact that I really weep in my heart on realizing that I continuously betray my Lord. For Judas it was 30 pieces of silver. For me the 30 pieces of silver have been converted into money and all sorts of articles. It breaks my heart when I realize that I have betrayed the Lord Jesus for a worthless thing. But how much I long to have Him alone as my treasure. Oh Lord, satisfy the deep desire of my heart. You are the only one I want to possess.

RESTITUTION—3

I was second in command at the place where I worked. At one time, my boss was to be absent for about 30 days and I was the one to handle the management of the office, which included the distribution of petrol. The petrol coupons were kept by the secretary. After some time, I asked her to give some to me for a certain amount. I used them on my personal car. But one night, when I went out with this car, it suddenly stopped somewhere and would no more start. All my efforts were in vain so I decided to leave the car where it was. It was the first time such a thing had ever happened to me. Another incident occurred that same night which obliged me to go and see an elder brother. Afterwards, I informed him of the problem I had had with the car. As I looked for the spiritual reason underlying this incident, my mind went to the petrol coupons I had taken from the secretary. This brother told me, "It was better for your boss to have been the one to give them to you."

Meanwhile, there was no apparent reason for me to blame myself. My boss was absent and I had taken the coupons through legal means. But my conscience kept troubling me about the matter. Immediately I arrived my office the following morning, I gave back the petrol coupons to the secretary.

Afterwards I went to look for a mechanic to tow the car from where I had left it the previous night. But just to be certain about what I was doing, I first went to where the car was parked. I was encouraged as I realized that at least it had not been stolen or broken into. Without much thought and without any hope at all, I nevertheless climbed into the car to give it another try. What a surprise I had to see the car start immediately! I could not believe it. I turned off the engine and began all over again, thinking that it had happened by chance. It started again. I was amazed. I drove it to the mechanic where I told him that despite all my efforts the previous night, the car had refused to start and that even though the car seemed to be in good working order, I would still want it to undergo a check-up. When I returned later on, the mechanic told me he had found nothing wrong with the engine.

For my part, I learnt the lesson! I understood how much God is concerned about my hands being always clean! It was enough for me to grasp God's desire for me. Oh! How I long to walk the pathway of integrity!

BACK MATTERS

<hr>

VERY IMPORTANT!!!

<hr>

If you have not yet received Jesus as your Lord and Saviour, I encourage you to receive Him. Here are some steps to help you,

ADMIT that you are a sinner by nature and by practice and that on your own you are without hope. Tell God you have personally sinned against Him in your thoughts, words and deeds. Confess your sins to Him, one after another in a sincere prayer. Do not leave out any sins that you can remember. Truly turn from your sinful ways and abandon them. If you stole, steal no more. If you have been committing adultery or fornication, stop it. God will not forgive you if you have no desire to stop sinning in all areas of your life, but if you are sincere, He will give you the power to stop sinning.

BELIEVE that Jesus Christ, who is God's Son, is the only Way, the only Truth and the only Life. Jesus said,

"I am the way, the truth and the life; no one comes to the Father, but by me" (John 14:6).

The Bible says,

"For there is one God, and there is one mediator between God and men, the man Christ Jesus, who gave himself as a ransom for all" (1 Timothy 2:5-6).

"And there is salvation in no one else (apart from Jesus), for there is no other name under heaven given among men by which we must be saved" (Acts 4:12).

But to all who received him, who believed in his name, he gave power to become children of God..." (John 1:12).

BUT,

CONSIDER the cost of following Him. Jesus said that all who follow Him must deny themselves, and this includes selfish financial, social and other interests. He also wants His followers to take up their crosses and follow Him. Are you prepared to abandon your own interests daily for those of Christ? Are you prepared to be led in a new direction by Him? Are you prepared to suffer for Him and die for Him if need be? Jesus will have nothing to do with half-hearted people. His demands are total. He will only receive and forgive those who are prepared to follow Him AT ANY COST. Think about it and count the cost. If you are prepared to follow Him, come what may, then there is something to do.

INVITE Jesus to come into your heart and life. He says,

"Behold I stand at the door and knock. If anyone hears my voice and opens the door (to his heart and life), I will come in to him and eat with him, and he with me" (Revelation 3:20).

Why don't you pray a prayer like the following one or one of your own construction as the Holy Spirit leads?

> "Lord Jesus, I am a wretched, lost sinner who
> has sinned in thought, word and deed.
> Forgive all my sins and cleanse me. Receive
> me, Saviour and transform me into a child
> of God. Come into my heart now and give
> me eternal life right now. I will follow you
> at all costs, trusting the Holy Spirit to give
> me all the power I need."

When you pray this prayer sincerely, Jesus answers at once and justifies you before God and makes you His child.

*Please write to us (**ztfbooks@cmfionline.org**) and I will pray for you and help you as you go on with Jesus Christ.*

THANK YOU

For Reading This Book

If you have any question and/or need help, do not hesitate to contact us through **ztfbooks@cmfionline.org**. If the book has blessed you, then we would also be grateful if you leave a positive review at your favorite retailer.

ZTF BOOKS, through the Book Ministry of Christian Missionary Fellowship International (CMFI) offers a wide selection of best selling Christian books (in print, eBook & audiobook formats) on a broad spectrum of topics, including marriage & family, sexuality, practical spiritual warfare, Christian service, Christian leadership, and much more. Visit us at **ztfbooks.com** to learn more about our latest releases and special offers. **And thank you for being a ZTF BOOK reader**.

We invite you to connect with more from the author through social media (**cmfionline**) and/or ministry website (**ztfministry.org**), where we offer both on-ground and remote training courses (all year round) from basic to university level at the **University of Prayer and Fasting (WUPF)** and the **School of Knowing and Serving God (SKSG)**. You are highly welcome to enrol at your soonest convenience. A **FREE online Bible Course** is also available.

We would like to recommend to you the next book in this series - Knowing God - The Greatest Need Of The Hour:

There are many believers today who worship "the unknown God". There are many who have never sought Him until He was revealed to them. There are many who do not know Him. There are many for whom sin is a wonderful attraction because they have never beheld the all-glorious face of the eternal Father nor heard His sweet voice. Their faith is more or less a theory. God seems absent or at best, withdrawn.

Do you know God?

When did you personally encounter Him? When was your last encounter with Him?

The greatest need of the hour is for saints who know God. This book is about knowing God. We consider that the greatest need of the hour is for believers to know their God and render to Him service that is an outflow of this knowledge and intimacy with Him. It is a book for you!

Professor Zacharias Tanee Fomum was born in the flesh on 20th June 1945 and became born again on 13th June 1956. On 1st October 1966, He consecrated his life to the Lord Jesus and to His service, and was filled with the Holy Spirit on 24th October 1970. He was taken to be with the Lord on 14th March, 2009.

Pr Fomum was admitted to a first class in the Bachelor of Science degree, graduating as a prize winning student from Fourah Bay College in the University of Sierra Leone in October 1969. At the age of 28, he was awarded a Ph.D. in Organic Chemistry by the University of Makerere, Kampala in Uganda. In October 2005, he was awarded a Doctor of Science (D.Sc) by the University of Durham, Great Britain. This higher doctorate was in recognition of his distinct contributions to scientific knowledge through research. As a Professor of Organic Chemistry in the University of Yaoundé 1, Cameroon, Professor Fomum supervised or co-supervised more than 100 Master's Degree and Doctoral Degree theses and co-authored over 160 scientific articles in leading international journals. He considered Jesus Christ the Lord of Science ("For by Him all things were created..." – Colossians 1:16), and scientific research an act of obedience to God's command to "subdue the earth" (Genesis 1:28). He therefore made the Lord Jesus the Director of his research laboratory while he took the place of deputy director, and attributed his outstanding success as a scientist to Jesus' revelational leadership.

In more than 40 years of Christian ministry, Pr Fomum travelled extensively, preaching the Gospel, planting churches and training spiritual leaders. He made more than:

- 700 missionary journeys within Cameroon, which ranged from one day to three weeks in duration.
- 500 missionary journeys to more than 70 different nations in all the six continents. These ranged from two days to six weeks in duration.

By the time of his going to be with the Lord in 2009, he had preached in over 1000 localities in Cameroon, sent over 200 national missionaries into many localities in Cameroon and planted over 1300 churches in the various administrative provinces of Cameroon. At his base in Yaoundé, he planted and built a mega-church with his co-workers which grew to a steady membership of about 12,000. Pr Fomum was the founding team-leader of Christian Missionary Fellowship International (CMFI); an evangelism, soul-winning, disciple making, Church-planting and missionary-sending movement with more than 200 international missionaries and thousands of churches in 65 nations spread across Africa, Europe, the Americas, Asia and Oceania. In the course of their ministry, Pr Fomum and his team witnessed more than 10,000 recorded healing miracles performed by God in answer to prayer in the name of Jesus Christ. These miracles include instant healings of headaches, cancers, HIV/AIDS, blindness, deafness, dumbness, paralysis, madness, and new teeth and organs received.

Pr Fomum read the entire Bible more than 60 times, read more than 1350 books on the Christian faith and authored over 150 books to advance the Gospel of Jesus Christ. 5 million copies of these books are in circulation in 12 languages as well as 16 million gospel tracts in 17 languages.

Pr Fomum was a man who sought God. He spent between 15 minutes and six hours daily alone with God in what he called Daily Dynamic Encounters with God (DDEWG). During these DDEWG he read God's Word, meditated on it, listened to God's voice, heard God speak to him, recorded what God was saying to him and prayed it through. He thus had over 18,000 DDEWG. He also had over 60 periods of withdrawing to seek God alone for periods that ranged from 3 to 21 days (which he termed Retreats for Spiritual Progress). The time he spent seeking God slowly transformed him into a man who hungered, thirsted and panted after God. His unceasing heart cry was: "Oh, that I would have more of God!"

Pr Fomum was a man of prayer and a leading teacher on prayer in many churches and conferences around the world. He considered prayer to be the most important work that can be done for God and for man. He was a man of faith who believed that God answers prayer. He kept a record of his prayer requests and had over 50, 000 recorded answers to prayer in his prayer books. He carried out over 100 Prayer Walks of between five and forty-seven kilometres in towns and cities around the world. He and his team carried out over 57 Prayer Crusades (periods of forty days and nights during which at least eight hours are invested into prayer each day). They also carried out over 80 Prayer Sieges (times of near non-stop praying that ranges from 24 hours to 120 hours). He authored the Prayer Power Series, a 13-volume set of books on various aspects of prayer; Supplication, Fasting, Intercession and Spiritual Warfare. He started prayer chains, prayer rooms, prayer houses, national and continental prayer movements in Cameroon and other nations. He worked with leaders of local churches in India to disciple and train more than 2 million believers.

Pr Fomum also considered fasting as one of the weapons of Christian Spiritual Warfare. He carried out over 250 fasts ranging from three days to forty days, drinking only water or water supplemented with soluble vitamins. Called by the Lord to a distinct ministry of intercession, he pioneered fasting and prayer movements and led in battles against principalities and powers obstructing the progress of the Gospel and God's global purposes. He was enabled to carry out 3 supra – long fasts of between 52 and 70 days in his final years.

Pr Fomum chose a lifestyle of simplicity and "self- imposed poverty" in order to invest more funds into the critical work of evangelism, soul winning, church-planting and the building up of believers. Knowing the importance of money and its role in the battle to reach those without Christ with the glorious Gospel, he and his wife grew to investing 92.5% of their earned income from all sources (salaries, allowances, royalties and cash gifts) into the Gospel. They invested with the hope that, as they grew in the knowledge and the love of the Lord, and the perishing souls of people, they would one day invest 99% of their income into the Gospel.

He was married to Prisca Zei Fomum and they had seven children who are all involved in the work of the Gospel, some serving as missionaries. Prisca is a national and international minister, specializing in the winning and discipling of children to Jesus Christ. She also communicates and imparts the vision of ministry to children with a view to raising and building up ministers to them.

The Professor owed all that he was and all that God had done through him, to the unmerited favour and blessing of God and to his worldwide army of friends and co-workers. He considered himself nothing without them and the blessing of God; and would have amounted to nothing but for them. All praise and glory to Jesus Christ!

facebook.com/cmfionline

twitter.com/cmfionline

instagram.com/cmfionline

pinterest.com/cmfionline

youtube.com/cmfionline

ALSO BY Z.T. FOMUM

https://ztfbooks.com

THE CHRISTIAN WAY

1. The Way Of Life
2. The Way Of Obedience
3. The Way Of Discipleship
4. The Way Of Sanctification
5. The Way Of Christian Character
6. The Way Of Spiritual Power
7. The Way Of Christian Service
8. The Way Of Spiritual Warfare
9. The Way Of Suffering For Christ
10. The Way Of Victorious Praying
11. The Way Of Overcomers
12. The Way Of Spiritual Encouragement
13. The Way Of Loving The Lord

THE PRAYER POWER SERIES

1. The Way Of Victorious Praying
2. The Ministry Of Fasting
3. The Art Of Intercession
4. The Practice Of Intercession
5. Praying With Power
6. Practical Spiritual Warfare Through Prayer
7. Moving God Through Prayer
8. The Ministry Of Praise And Thanksgiving

PRACTICAL HELPS FOR OVERCOMERS

LEADING GOD'S PEOPLE

GOD, SEX AND YOU

OFF-SERIES

PRACTICAL HELPS IN SANCTIFICATION

15. Rebellion

MAKING SPIRITUAL PROGRESS

1. The Ministers And The Ministry of The New Covenant
2. The Cross In The Life And Ministry Of The Believer
3. Making Spiritual Progress, Volume 1
4. Making Spiritual Progress, Volume 2
5. Making Spiritual Progress, Volume 3
6. Making Spiritual Progress, Volume 4
7. Moving on With The Lord Jesus Christ
8. The Narrow Way (Volume 1)
9. Making Spiritual Progress (Volumes 1-4)

EVANGELISM

1. 36 Reasons For Winning The Lost To Christ
2. Soul Winning, Volume 1
3. Soul Winning, Volume 2
4. The Winning of The Lost as Life's Supreme Task
5. Salvation And Soul-Winning
6. Soul Winning And The Making Of Disciples
7. <u>Victorious Soul-Winning</u>

GOD LOVES YOU

1. God's Love And Forgiveness
2. The Way Of Life
3. Come Back Home My Son; I Still Love You

4. Jesus Loves You And Wants To Heal You
5. Come And See; Jesus Has Not Changed!
6. Celebrity A Mask
7. Encounter The Saviour
8. Meet The Liberator
9. Jesus Saves And Heals Today
10. Jesus is The Answer

WOMEN OF THE GLORY

1. **The Secluded Worshipper: Prophetess Anna**
2. **Unending Intimacy: Mary of Bethany**
3. **Winning Love: Mary Magdalene**

ZTF COMPLETE WORKS

1. The School of Soul Winners and Soul Winning
2. The Complete Works of Z.T.F on Holiness (Volume 1)
3. The Complete Works of Z.T.F on Basic Christian Doctrine
4. The Complete Works of Z.T.F on Marriage (Volume 1)
5. The Complete Works of Z.T.F on The Gospel Message (Volume 1)
6. The Complete Works of Z.T.F on Prayer (Volume 1)
7. The Complete Works of Z.T.F on Prayer (Volume 2)
8. The Complete Works of Z.T.F on Prayer (Volume 3)
9. The Complete Works of Z.T.F on Prayer (Volume 4)
10. The Complete Works of Z.T.F on Prayer (Volume 5)
11. The Complete Works of Z.T.F on Leadership (Volume 1)

SPECIAL SERIES

ZTF AUTO-BIOGRAPHIES

THE OVERTHROW OF PRINCIPALITIES

3. The Prophecy of the Overthrow of The Satanic Prince of Yaounde
4. The Prophecy of the Overthrow of The Satanic Prince of Douala
5. The overthrow of principalities and powers
6. From His Lips: The Battles He Fought

CONTINUOUS PERSONAL SPIRITUAL REVIVAL

1. Victorious Proclamations

OTHER BOOKS

1. The Missionary as a Son
2. What Our Ministry is
3. Conserver la Moisson
4. Disciples of Jesus Christ to Make Disciples For Jesus Christ
5. The House Church in God's Eternal Purposes
6. Christian Maturation
7. Heroes of the Kingdom
8. Spiritual Leadership in the Pattern of Gideon
9. The School of Evangelism
10. A Good Minister of Jesus Christ
11. Building a Spiritual Nation: The Foundation
12. Building a Spiritual Nation: Spiritual Statesmanship
13. Removing Obstacles Through Prayer and Fasting
14. The Chronicles of Our Ministry
15. The Making of Disciples: The Master's Way

DISTRIBUTORS OF ZTF BOOKS

These books can be obtained in French and English Language from any of the following distribution outlets:

EDITIONS DU LIVRE CHRETIEN (ELC)

- **Location:** Paris, France
- **Email:** editionlivrechretien@gmail.com
- **Phone:** +33 6 98 00 90 47

INTERNET

- **Location:** on all major online **eBook, Audiobook** and **print-on-demand** (paperback) retailers.
- **Email**: ztfbooks@cmfionline.org
- **Phone**: +47 454 12 804
- **Website**: ztfbooks.com

CPH YAOUNDE

- **Location:** Yaounde, Cameroon
- **Email:** editionsztf@gmail.com
- **Phone:** +237 74756559

ZTF LITERATURE AND MEDIA HOUSE

- **Location:** Lagos, Nigeria
- **Email:** zlmh@ztfministry.org
- **Phone:** +2348152163063

CPH BURUNDI

- **Location:** Bujumbura, Burundi
- **Email:** cph-burundi@ztfministry.org
- **Phone:** +257 79 97 72 75

CPH UGANDA

- **Location:** Kampala, Uganda
- **Email:** cph-uganda@ztfministry.org
- **Phone:** +256 785 619613

CPH SOUTH AFRICA

- **Location:** Johannesburg, RSA
- **Email:** tantohtantoh@yahoo.com
- **Phone:** +27 83 744 5682